THE
THRIVAL
GUIDE

Also by Eric Eaton

The Raging Sloth

THE THRIVAL GUIDE

A PRACTICAL PATH TO INTENTIONAL LIVING IN A CONSUMER DRIVEN, TECH-SATURATED, AND DISTRACTED WORLD

ERIC EATON

ISBN: 1-64085-124-5

ISBN-13: 978-1-64085-124-5

Library of Congress Control Number: 2018933985

Author Academy Elite, Powell, OH

The Internet addresses in this book are accurate at the time of publication. They are provided as a resource. Eric Eaton and the publisher do not endorse them or vouch for their content or permanence.

To protect the privacy of those who have shared their stories with the author, some details and names have been changed.

Photography: Rebecca Ofstedahl – Third Eye Photography

Cover Design: Dissect Designs – DissectDesigns.com

For Erica, Dylan, Jude, & Presley:
Thank you for pushing me
to live my dreams!

CONTENTS

Stop Surviving

Eliminate Distractions

Start Thriving

INTRODUCTION

"As tough an idea as it often is to stomach, the best way to thrive in a world that requires grunt work is to stop seeing it as grunt work." ~ Ryan Holiday

"I'm surviving!"

This is the typical response to benign greetings that usually begin with "How are you?" But when you truly ponder this question, is *surviving* your main goal in life? When you come to the end of your life, is your greatest aspiration to have the words "I Survived!" engraved on your headstone?

Life is not something we hope to survive. We survive circumstances, challenges, a zombie apocalypse, or Christmas with the in-laws. Survival is living through a 4-a.m. shopping spree on Black Friday in Wal-Mart. Survival is how we get through challenging circumstances in life, not how we hope to *live* life.

Life itself is meant for so much more. Life is meant to be awesome, extraordinary, and impactful. Yet too often we are content to live a lackluster life stuck in survival mode.

I was going to write about wilderness survival, but then I realized the topic would be too easy. Basically, you need to find food, shelter...and don't die. Now before survivalist like Bear Grylls begin to hunt me down, I'm kidding. Besides, you don't want to take my advice on wilderness survival—wilderness survival is much more suited to survivalists like Grylls. But there's something simplistic and minimalistic about wilderness survival, which seems attractive. When you're out in the woods, all the excesses of life are stripped away, and you spend your time concentrating on what matters most: keeping yourself alive.

What used to simply be called "life" or the way of living before modern technology, has become a specialized skill. One where we use vacation time and pay a survivalist an enormous amount of money to teach us how to survive in the wild so that we can traipse around the woods for a week.

The irony is we are willing to pay big bucks for a survivalist to teach us how to live a week each year in the wild. Yet we would never think about seeking out someone to teach us how to live the other 51 weeks of the year with some type of purpose, intention, and mission.

Compare the old way of living to our modern, chaotic, and overloaded lives. There are hundreds of wilderness survival books and manuals out there, which the majority of people will never read, by the way. But there are very few, if any, guides on how to successfully navigate your modern life. Not just to survive and keep your head above water, but to truly thrive, to live an exceptional life—one with purpose and meaning.

This is why I didn't write a survival guide for the modern world, but a Thrival Guide. Because unlike the wilderness, the point is more than to just stay alive. We were made to THRIVE.

The challenge to thriving is understanding the unique times we live in—where culture, technology, society, philosophy, and thought are evolving at an exponential rate. Yet we don't take the time to learn how to absorb, understand, and process all the information and rapidly evolving ideas around us.

We're being bombarded with numerous messages telling us to live a better life, make millions, find success, and do whatever we want to do. But we feel stuck and unable to take the first step toward these goals, because we have no idea how to effectively face the many obstacles in our lives.

If you are honest, then you know you're probably only surviving parts of your life. But why shouldn't you be thriving in *all* parts of your life? Your inability to thrive usually comes down to the lack of necessary skills needed in these modern times. Changes are happening faster than your ability to adapt or understand how to use them or how they affect your life.

I'm still learning how to thrive after 20 years of trial and error. Mostly error, when it comes to attempting to live a thriving life in the midst of chronic pain. I thought I could live like everyone else but was failing miserably in my career, life, and relationships due to my pain. Once I eventually learned a process to live effectively in pain, I began to see all the other issues affecting my life; such as overwhelming distractions, constantly changing technology, and the realization I had no skills or coping mechanisms to deal with any of these problems appropriately.

I was tired of just surviving life, leaving my destiny to chance, and hoping for the best. I wanted to take the bull by the horns and make the most of what was given to me, regardless of the pain I was in, the circumstances I faced, or the challenges in front of me. I was no longer content to survive. I was ready to thrive!

To begin with, I was going to have to take a step back and see how I got to this place in my life, identify the distractions I was facing, and create a clear path to a Thrival Life. The road was not easy but an extremely enlightening one as I learned about the numerous stresses that affected my life. Some without me even realizing the impact they were having on my day-to-day living.

This guide was created to offer you a roadmap to the Thrival Life. The Thrival Life is living life with all the fervor and passion you possess. But this type of living has somehow been lost over the last few generations. Now is the time to take our lives back.

In this book, you will learn the answers to these questions:

- Where did our problems come from?

- How did we deal with our problems historically?

- How are we letting our problems be a detriment to our current lives?

- How can we begin to take back control of our lives?

- What distractions are keeping us from living a thriving life?

- How do we accept our great Thrival Adventure and live the life we desire?

We will begin the process by taking a step back and identifying those areas of your life where you struggle and have stress. Identify the many distractions you're currently facing. Then slowly begin the process of walking out of the muck and mire of life into an adventure that is uniquely your own.

Throughout this book, there exists varying degrees of help, content, and advice. If a certain chapter is not applicable, then feel free to move on to the next. Let the other messages throughout the book permeate your life for a true transformation.

Begin today to truly live a Thrival Life beyond the survivalist mentality of our modern world.

PART 1

LACK OF PERSONAL PREPARATION

1

THE EVOLUTION OF OUR MODERN PROBLEMS

How Did We Get Here?

"Do not anticipate trouble or worry over what may never happen. Keep in the sunlight."
~ Marcus Aurelius

I often think about statements my children say to me, which would have been completely lost on my father when I was their age. Statements like "Dad, just Google it!", "Check your phone!", or my favorite, "I'm tweeting!" If I had said any of these phrases to my father, I'm pretty sure I would have been stared at blankly or would have never seen the light of day again, or I would have been ruthlessly interrogated to understand the meaning of these strange words. But I do believe if I were to tell my dad I learned something on Facebook, at least he might have thought I was reading at the library!

In one generation, our vernacular has drastically changed. Not because of some disconnect between

3

the generations but all due to the introduction of different technology. Our lives have literally been turned inside out in less than 20 years. Yet we are supposed to keep on track without missing a beat.

Contrary to popular belief, these modern times did not magically appear. But they did evolve at a rapid pace. With the accelerated development of technology, science, thoughts, ideas, and ideology, our ability to understand how these areas fit congruently and precisely into our lives has lagged behind. Many of the struggles we face have evolved out of this rapid progress into our modern lives. Our problems, issues, stressors, and challenges are changing much quicker than our ability to adapt to the circumstances.

This is why it's important to start our journey with the understanding of how we got here. The process of moving from a slow-paced tech-free life, to a fast-paced tech-inundated society. With this understanding, we will begin to see how these circumstances are directly affecting our lives. Then make the correct steps to begin to live a thriving life.

Historical Problems

As recent as 200-300 years ago, people grew up in a village or town, and problems would have been localized to roughly a 15-mile radius. The world's problems didn't matter, and thus did not exist beyond the boundaries of your city walls or borders. You had no way of knowing what was happening outside your community unless a visitor came through town. Your major concerns would have been war, famine, clothing, shelter, the growing and harvest seasons, and weather. The basics of simply living life.

Even within these small villages, the idea of comparison was very limited. You only had to be the brightest, prettiest, strongest, or most capable in the town. If you were competing in any arena, it was localized to your small community. Contrast this competition to today's arena where you're comparing your abilities and competing against the brightest, prettiest, strongest, and most capable in the *world*.

Our world lived within this limited construct for thousands of years. Very little change occurred over the course of this time period—with the exception of the Renaissance, the Enlightenment, or the Industrial Revolution. Progress was extremely slow and usually met with strong resistance.

Because the changes were slow, society and individuals were able to adapt to the situation or circumstances with little obstruction to their lives. For instance, simple changes like crop rotations or better irrigation made it easier to work the farm. Back then, our adaptation to new circumstances, which were minimal and slow-paced, allowed us the ability to still thrive regardless of our stage in life.

Slingshot into Modern Problems

We have catapulted ourselves into the modern arena—if you look at it from a historical standpoint, this massive change has taken place over a relatively short period of time. The shift from our historical problems and modern problems are also exponentially growing with no end in sight.

Think about how technology, culture, and thought have advanced and shifted in the last twenty years alone. Historically, a timeframe of twenty years wasn't enough to make any significant difference in global progression. For thousands of years, people lived their entire lives with limited or no change directly affecting them. Yet most of us cannot even conceive of what life will look like twenty years from now.

The rapid evolution of thought and technology is compounded by how much information is available and the quantities of data we consume. On a daily basis, we are inundated with information far beyond what we can consume or even comprehend. Our heads are constantly spinning with fifty different insights into the same topic... not fully knowing what or which fact to believe.

Studies have shown that a typical social media user consumes 285 pieces of content daily, which equates to an eye-opening 54,000 words, and for the truly active, as many as 1,000 clickable links.

A study from the UK revealed that everyone is bombarded by the equivalent of 174 newspapers of data a day. The growth in the Internet, 24-hour television, and mobile phones mean we now consume five times as much information every day as we did in 1986.

Think about your information consumption for a moment. You're consuming five times the amount of information you did thirty years ago. I don't care who you are—your mind has not evolved quickly enough to consume five times the amount of information in only thirty years. I still can't figure out how to use my Instagram account, and I have had it for several years. As we attempt to digest the massive amounts of information being consumed, eventually something has to give.

In very basic terms, we're attempting to use a compass that no longer works to keep navigating our modern world. The evolution of ideas and ways of living have been very disproportionate to our ability to update and adapt. The effect is we are becoming overwhelmed, frustrated, insecure, stressed out, and ultimately, we cover our lives with worry. The idea of thriving is becoming an ancient pursuit no longer relevant in these times.

Analysis Paralysis

This inundation of information has begun to create a rising discomfort in our lives. We can identify the discomfort borne out of the mind-numbing analysis, but we don't know how to label the exact feeling. Up until recent history, there have been very few accounts of individuals suffering from what we term as *analysis paralysis*. As little as two centuries ago, an individual would have been considered privileged if they ever held a single book—let alone gorged themselves with information.

Analysis paralysis is a situation where people have too much information to digest to allow them to solve a problem. So they freeze and do nothing. Yet this analysis paralysis is a situation many of us find ourselves floundering in on a constant basis.

This information overload has taxed our mental and emotional state. In the past, if you wanted a cow, wheat, food, or a new cart, you only needed to go to the one person in town who has that particular item and buy what they had. Not a whole lot of decision-making to do, except knowing whether you want the said item or not. You didn't have the option to drive down the street to see if you could get a better deal on wheat, get a different brand of milk, or find a spotted cow instead of a brown cow.

Compare this scenario to one specific category in today's world. If you go to your local supermarket, there's a whole aisle dedicated to breakfast cereal. Depending upon your supermarket, you'll probably face over 100 different types of cereal. This would be fine, if picking a new cereal was the only major decision you had to make in life.

But when, on top of your cereal choices, you add other decisions to make, such as with cars, clothing, furniture, children's activities, colleges, careers, or what's for dinner, you can become overwhelmed easily—not only do you have to make a decision in each of these areas, but it has to be an informed one.

I know I have been in this place many times, like when I wanted to buy a grill. I spent massive amounts of time researching what makes a great grill—the number of burners, the BTU output, and how large of a grilling area I have space for. In a short period of time, I was attempting to become a grill guru. I finally got to the point where I went out and purchased the best grill I could buy for the money. Yet, as soon as I got home, I stressed and fretted about it, thinking, "Did I make the right decision?"

Having access to more information doesn't necessarily calm my fears. Instead, it can cause me to worry more than I should over trivial items and issues that don't deserve this type of dedication and intensity, such as buying a grill.

What to Do with Worry?

Historically, worry was not a bad feeling, it was given to us as an emotional response—a way to heighten our senses to ensure we were safe from some predator or danger. In a later chapter, we will unwrap the purpose of worry and its accompanying issues, but for now, we'll tackle how to deal with worry in these modern times, especially when we kick it into overdrive.

Worry is a response to ambiguity we experience. It is basically our attempt to find a solution or add clarity and purpose to a confusing, threatening, or foggy situation in our lives.

The good part of worry is it gets your mind moving to be creative in solving problems. The bad part of worry is when you cannot solve the problem, it evolves into anxiety and stress.

Knowing we can't just set all our problems aside and ignore their effects, what do we do with worry in our lives? This is a question we will unravel. For as long as we live in a state of worry, we are living a life in survival mode, thus limiting our options in pursuing the Thrival Life!

2

THE UNFORESEEN OBSTACLES

Identifying Modern-Day Problems

"Engineers like to solve problems. If there are no problems handily available, they will create their own problems." ~ Scott Adams

As a parent, I feel I have taken all of my children's changes and adaptions as they have grown in stride. I like to think I have been prepared for every issue and problem my wife and I have faced thus far. Except one: teaching them how to drive! Why did no one ever tell me this would be the most frightening experience of not only parenting but my entire life? Who thought it was a good idea to give a 15-year-old control of a 3,000-pound vehicle?

Whether it was teaching Dylan to drive a stick shift over two mountain passes in one day (probably my poor judgment), or Jude slamming on the gas instead of the brakes and blowing through an intersection—which was thankfully empty; otherwise he would have plowed through everything like pins at a bowling alley—I don't think there's enough aromatherapy, essential oils, or scented candles that could calm me down after constantly seeing my life flash before my eyes.

There were times when I'd get home and step out of the car mumbling unintelligible words and bouncing around like a giant blow-up figure in front of a car dealership. The stress I experienced in those moments was off the charts. Until I'd remember I have to teach *three* teenagers three years in a row, and my stress levels would go through the roof.

Teaching my children to drive has made me aware that stress can come from the most unexpected places. Are you aware of the stresses that fill your life? For the most part, you're very familiar with finances, family, health, or the effects of an unhealthy job environment. But there is a myriad of other stressors hovering around you, which you largely ignore.

Our culture is literally swimming in a pool of stress and anxiety with each of us floating around frantically trying to keep our heads above water. These stress-causing manifestations are unlabeled and swept under the rug, so we don't give them the attention they need to alleviate them from our lives.

We're going to take a look at all the different issues, challenges, and obstacles most of us face in our lives. The purpose of this exercise is not to raise an alarm, but to open our eyes to all of the intricate stress-inducing pieces of our lives. By identifying each one specifically, we then have the choice to lighten them or to remove them altogether.

The 5-E Problems

Problems come in all shapes and sizes—from spilled milk at breakfast to a life-changing car wreck on the way to work. With each type of problem comes varying levels of control over the situation and the amount of stress each circumstance creates in our lives. For most people, they have never taken the time to figure out what problems they have in their lives and the amount of stress these problems are causing.

Most of our problems can be categorized into five different areas. Each problem has three levels of control we have over the situation, and three levels of stress the problem emits. We're going to take a closer look at the 5-E problems and break them down in order to better understand how to categorize them in our own lives.

The 5-E Problems

Types of Problems	Amount of Control	Stress Level
External Problems	Limited Control	Medium Stress
Extension Problems	Varying Control	High Stress
Expectation Problems	Varying Control	High Stress
Emergency Problems	Limited Control	High Stress
Everyday Problems	Total Control	Low Stress

External Problems

The first group of problems to discuss is the External Problems. These are the global, national, or local issues you read about, face, or are exposed to on a daily basis. You have limited or absolutely no control over them, yet they still cause stress and anxiety in your life. Whenever you see an earthquake or flood hit a part of the country you do not live in or a tsunami on the other side of the world, you can't help but feel sad and have the desire to help.

With the advent of social media, these types of issues now have the ability to escalate your stress. Before social media existed and a terrible event occurred in the news, you would feel sad, but would not fixate on the issue. Now, when something happens, you see it plastered all over social media and on 24-hour news channels. You may even personally know people affected by the disaster because of your social media feed.

One such example is the aftermath of Hurricane Harvey in Texas. My sister shared a picture of her in-laws' house in Houston partially submerged under three feet of water. Even though the hurricane did not directly affect my family, the reality of seeing childhood friends' and other people's struggles was overwhelming. With the onslaught of coverage, you begin to feel guilty and want to help, but may not know how or have the ability to respond.

Now don't get me wrong—the initial feeling of wanting to reach out is the correct response. You should want to help and provide aid to those around you who are in need. The problem is we cannot help everyone in every situation. Updating your Facebook feed with pictures or images of the event would be a full-time job, with all the disasters happening in the world. When you can't help everyone in every situation, you end up feeling guilty for doing nothing.

These external problems manifest themselves in the form of terrorism, the global economy, environmental issues, wars, famine, disease, and natural disasters. These are relevant issues that exist in your life and which people think about on a constant basis. A survey in *Business Insider* revealed the top 10 issues people in America are most concerned about.

1. Climate change and destruction of natural resources (45.2%)

2. Large scale conflict and wars (38.5%)

3. Religious conflicts (33.8%)

4. Poverty (31.1%)

5. Government accountability, transparency, and corruption (21.7%)

6. Safety, security, and well-being (18.1%)

7. Lack of education (16.5%)

8. Lack of political freedom and political instability (15.5%)

9. Food and water security (15.1%)

10. Lack of economic opportunity and unemployment (14.2%)

When you look at the list, it is startling to realize that with most of the issues mentioned, you can't directly affect, change, or improve them with your actions alone. Sure, you can do your part to help with climate change, poverty, or government corruption. But in reality, most of these would require an organized movement to effect change and turn the tide.

These External Problems need to be recognized for what they are in your life. Admit to yourself you cannot be everywhere at every time to help everyone, and that is perfectly fine. Give yourself grace in your own existence. Find the issues or causes you do believe in, and then invest fully. Pray and help out where and whenever you can, but don't let the condition of the world, which is outside of your control, become a barrier to your own thriving life.

Extension Problems

Extension Problems are the next set of problems we constantly face. These are local problems affecting us directly, but we have little say or control over them, and we still may be at the mercy of others for real change to happen.

The Extension Problems can be national, state, or local issues, such as taxes, riots, politics, immigration, national debt, parking, traffic, cost of living, local drug problems, lack of time, and many more. Depending upon their severity, these problems can cause a drastic shift in our lives.

A survey from ABC News noted Americans worry most about the following:

1. 54% - The availability and affordability of healthcare

2. 53% - The economy

3. 51% - The possibility of future terrorist attacks in the U.S.

4. 46% - The Social Security system

5. 46% - The size and power of the federal government

6. 46% - The way income and wealth are distributed in the U.S.

7. 43% - Hunger and homelessness

8. 43% - Crime and violence

9. 39% - Illegal immigration

10. 38% - Drug use

11. 37% - Unemployment

12. 34% - The quality of the environment

13. 28% - The availability and affordability of energy

14. 28% - Race relations

15. 25% - Climate change

Hunger, crime, immigration, and rising racial tensions are all on the forefront of Americans' worries. While you might have control over drugs, crime, and violence by moving to another neighborhood, other items like immigration, unemployment, or the economy will follow you no matter where you live in the U.S. Many Americans are expending a tremendous amount of energy worrying about their finances, employment, and whether they can afford healthcare.

The anxiety these situations create is ever present in many people's lives, causing an underlying stress which is difficult to identify but can have subtle effects on health and well-being.

The recent rise of unstable race relations is a good example. The majority of people want a better outcome regardless of race. They want a better result than what we are seeing. But very few reasonable and viable strategies to achieve this goal have been offered, or the strategies are across the spectrum of what might be a workable solution. The end result is an underlying stress among all races which are living with tension because of thinly defined solutions.

The race issue can be duplicated when it comes to immigration, the economy, or local crime. You need to be able to identify stresses in your life and the effect they're having on your emotional health, especially if you have little control over the outcome of the situation.

Expectation Problems

Expectation Problems have far more weight than people give credit for, and they can have a profound influence on your life. They can also come from a variety of sometimes unexpected sources.

Each year at camp, in a grand ceremony, I get the awesome task of dressing up from helmet to boots as a knight. I then mount a grand steed and ride in a majestic display to lay my sword upon the campers' shoulders to knight them. However, the first year we attempted the ceremony, it didn't quite look as majestic as I'd imagined.

That year, we were so busy attempting to figure out all the logistics of camp, the planning of the closing ceremony got pushed to the back burner. During camp, I went to a costume shop to rent their only "knight" outfit, which was made of plastic and coated in gray spray paint. Later, I went down to the stables of the Boy Scout Camp we were camping at and secured a fine steed for my grand adventure. I was assured my horse would be fit for a king.

In my head I was thinking this was going to blow the socks off the boys. I would ride in a majestic display reminiscent of King Arthur, decked out in knightly glory. Well, this image was short-lived. First off, the stable didn't bring me a fine steed, but a rather small and seemingly frail horse. A horse so small he looked like he came from a miniature farm. The knight costume hung awkwardly in all the wrong places, and I couldn't get the pieces secured tightly around my body. I looked more like Don Quixote on a small donkey riding off to battle windmills than a noble knight.

To make matters worse, when I did get on the horse, he let out a bellow, which I interpreted as, "Whoa, you're way too heavy!" He was used to small Boy Scouts riding him all day, not a large man wearing a knight outfit from a Monty Python skit. Alas, the ceremony went well and the boys were awestruck by the entire event, even though it did not live up to *my* expectations.

You can probably remember an event or time in your life when you had great expectations about how a situation was supposed to turn out. But through circumstances beyond your control, the results might have concluded in a very different way. You can probably recount the anger, frustration, sadness, or depression that might have ensued from an unmet expectation.

We live with these expectations all around us and are usually frustrated when things don't go our way. Yet we never take the time to process how these unmet expectations are affecting our feelings, emotions, or temper. Over time, these emotions will snowball enough until we eventually have an avalanche of pent-up anger or frustration erupting seemingly out of nowhere.

These expectations can be around relationships (spouse, children, parents, boss, co-workers, and friends), jobs, houses, cars, looks, clothes, kids' activities, living your dream, and any of a hundred other things. When reality does not meet the image we've conjured in our head, we usually drown in frustration or disappointment. The irony is, your job, house, looks, or relationships could be just fine, but since they didn't meet your defined expectations, the results are considered failures. This constant emotional and mental struggle can bring even the strongest of individuals to their knees.

Identifying the sources of these expectations can be challenging because they can stem from many places. While expectations mainly come from within yourself, they may be influenced by other sources long before you develop awareness. Expectations can materialize from traditions, parents, spouses, social media, social expectations, culture, a coach, teacher, or even movies or stories which have captured your attention.

You can relate this issue back to your historical problems. In days gone past, you only had to be the best or the most beautiful in your village or town. Now this expectation has gone global by comparison. You're no longer only comparing your ability to the person down the block, but also to the person on the other side of the country or world, which is completely unachievable. The unrealistic expectations you're placing upon yourself is monstrous. Even when you know you're comparing, it's difficult to step back and not get sucked into this cycle.

You need to be very cognizant of the expectations you're placing on yourself. Are they healthy expectations, which cause growth? Or unhealthy expectations, which cause you to chase unrealistic pursuits? Attempting to achieve unhealthy expectations will always result in living a life set in survival mode.

Emergency Problems

Emergency Problems are specific problems which come out of nowhere, and you have limited or no control over them...and yet they can cause a tremendous amount of stress and anxiety in your life. These problems can be as simple as a car breaking down on the way to work or as major as a heart attack. Either way, they certainly cause a disruption in your day and life.

The Emergency Problems are usually major stressors in your life no matter how large or small. They can come in the form of unexpected health issues, accidents, family crisis, job layoffs, marital problems, or moving to a new town, death, trauma, or even living through a natural disaster.

The American Physiological Association, noting the stress caused by hurricane victims, stated, "It is common for people to experience very strong emotional reactions with the arrival of a hurricane and its accompanying damage to homes and community infrastructures." They continued, "If possible, avoid major life decisions such as switching jobs because these activities tend to be highly stressful."

In the situation of a hurricane—and three have hit the U.S. while I was writing this chapter—it's easy to dismiss your own thoughts and emotions because many people are currently affected with something much worse. *Why should I be stressed*, you ask yourself, *when others are suffering the same situation or worse?* But living through the devastation and rebuilding is highly stressful for a multitude of reasons. You cannot discount the emotional and stressful toll it will take on you.

While there is very little anyone can do to prepare for these types of events, it's important to understand your own health and stress during these particular times. What can you do to avoid adding any more pressure or stress in the situation? How can you essentially take a higher view of the circumstances in order to sail through them more gracefully?

These are the times in your life where you simply need to hang on and ride the wave as gracefully as possible. Give yourself enough grace to remain in survival mode for a time, but take specific steps to move back into a Thrival Life.

Everyday Problems

Everyday Problems are the simple road bumps we experience on a consistent basis, such as paying bills, traffic, yard work, chores, buying clothes, dealing with an angry boss, having a disjointed job, or driving your children all over the state for their games, meets, and competitions.

Most of these are minor and can be dealt with accordingly. Yet many get stacked upon each other at one time, creating quite a burden.

Look at one area of your life and the stresses your job can put on you. The following list contains recorded effects of stress that individuals have incurred from their jobs alone.

- Being unhappy in your job
- Having a heavy workload or too much responsibility
- Working long hours
- Having poor management, unclear expectations of your work, or having no say in the decision-making process
- Working under dangerous conditions
- Being insecure about your chance for advancement or risk of termination
- Having to give speeches in front of colleagues
- Facing discrimination or harassment at work, especially if your company isn't supportive

You add in your finances, paying bills, fixing the car, finding a competent repairman, or an overloaded kid's schedule...there is a very thin line being walked. These are the first-world problems many who live in any modern culture will face.

While we can admit they're usually the result of a luxury—like complaining of your car breaking down (couldn't we just be happy we have the resources to own a car?)—this rationalization usually doesn't help our anxiety when we're stranded on the side of the road with a flat tire in a rainstorm and with no cell service.

The natural response to many of these problems will be to hunker down in a guarded position to survive the storm. The better solution is to face these problems head on and deal with them appropriately.

Carrying a Heavy Load

Individually, most of these problems can be handled in stride. It becomes an issue when they keep getting stacked upon one another.

Think of yourself pushing a wheelbarrow down the road. As you're pushing, people keep putting pieces of wood into the wheelbarrow. Each piece of wood, in and of itself, is inconsequential. You could go for a long time with the individual pieces. But the farther you go down the road, the more your wheelbarrow keeps getting loaded down.

Eventually, you'll realize you can no longer push the wheelbarrow any further. It's too heavy. Confusion sinks in, because you don't know how you got to this point. You don't know how to move forward, or what to do with the massive load you have accumulated in your wheelbarrow. But no matter how hard you try, you can't push your load anymore.

This is how stress, pain, and anxiety begin to mount up in our life. Unfortunately, all too often we find ourselves in this place after a painful realization—and by then we think it's too late.

If you don't move any further, you'll simply end up sitting down by your wheelbarrow, attempting to figure out how you can survive at the barest minimum. The other option is to get creative so you're not weighed down by the burdens of life and thus can truly thrive.

3

DEVIATING FROM THE TRAIL

The Results of Modern Problems

"Life is not about waiting for the storms to pass.
It's about learning how to dance in the rain."
~ Vivian Greene

Taking the road less traveled is our preference when it comes to family vacations. And by less traveled, I'm referring to the roads that are less crowded and generally offer us a much better scenic ride. The problem with this course of action is attempting to find the right road to travel.

On one trip, we were returning from San Francisco back to Colorado and wanted to stay off the major roads. The western part of the United States has some beautiful countryside, and we wanted to take in as much scenery as possible. When we came to one junction, we took the road we thought was correct and kept on cruising. About thirty minutes later, my wife and I began to get a little concerned—nothing specific we could point out, only something didn't seem right.

When we were able to get to a place with cell service, we looked back at our map only to realize we'd taken the wrong road. We had to turn the car around and drive another thirty minutes back to the junction in order to get back on track. We added another hour to an already long day of driving.

When you deviate from the trail, there will always be consequences. Sometimes, we unknowingly wander from our path, but nevertheless, we still have to understand where our path is taking us and whether it's the right direction.

When you begin to understand how culture has evolved and how rapidly this evolution has progressed, you'll also understand how easy it is to deviate from the trail. Then you compact the stress these circumstances are causing by either attempting to keep up or stay on the trail. The reality then becomes more evident as to the reason why we have left the trail and the issues it has caused.

We have been deviating off the trail of a thriving life for many years now, and what we're only now beginning to understand are the problems these deviations are causing on us as individuals and as a community. We have been buying into myths about how we should be living. While it's not certain where these myths originated, the harm they're causing us in living a thriving life is undeniable.

Information Overload

Knowledge is good. Information, on the other hand, may not always be worthwhile. While most of us may not be able to discern between the two, it's important to understand that there's a difference between each term. Knowledge helps you grow, learn, and become an overall better person. Information is just that—information. It may or may not have any effect on your life, and in the long run may actually cause you harm.

A New York Times article stated the average American consumes 34 gigabytes of content and 100,000 words of information in a single day. This doesn't mean we read 100,000 words a day—it means that 100,000 words cross our eyes and ears in a single 24-hour period. The information comes through various channels, including the television, radio, the Web, text messages, and video games.

Because of our global 24-hour news, we have inserted ourselves into every conflict, war, famine, political situation, environmental and terrorist act happening all over the world. Even though we don't have any control over these circumstances, and most of these situations have no direct bearing on our lives, they're still causing us stress. Plus, the more sensationalized the news, the better the story, and the more attention it gets.

What you have to realize is 24-hour news services don't care about giving you an informed decision. They're a for-profit business and are mainly concerned about ratings. If they only showed puppies playing with unicorns under rainbows and no one watched, they would be out of business. Thus, in their pursuit of ratings, they simply regurgitate any type of information they can in order to keep your eyes glued to their station.

Through social media, Internet news, and 24-hour cable news, we set ourselves up to be constant consumers of useless information. The canvas of information is being painted with extremely broad strokes covering up the details, and the picture eventually becomes meaningless.

We also add to our confusion by not knowing who to believe when there are five different views and opinions of the same statement or story—and all given through each individual's bias.

We're trapped by our technology that constantly sends updates to stories which have no bearing on our lives, and in turn, we get angry, frustrated, or bitter in response to the content. The resulting information overload causes stress and anxiety in ways we don't even realize, and this deviates us from the trail of a Thrival Life. The farther we get away from the path of a thriving life, the more we hunker down to survive.

I Need My Technology

To further throw us off course, we believe we must have our technology. We have been told this myth since the moment technology first knocked on our door. With Henry Ford's Assembly Line, we were going to be able to make things faster, more efficient, and more productive. While technology has provided us with a tremendous amount of progress, luxuries, and the world at our fingertips, we can barely keep up with all of the advances bursting on the scene every day.

But if we are truly honest, the overload of technology has complicated our lives. The faster technology is being delivered, the less time we have to see its true benefits as it applies to our specific needs—let alone accurately research where a particular technology might fit into our lives. Most of the time, we purchase items because it looks cool or our neighbors own the latest model, bragging about how it has changed their lives. Or even that the general population is purchasing gadgets, and we don't want to be left behind.

The most glaring side effect is the fact we are becoming more distracted than ever. We have to constantly be on the lookout for new technology and whether it is a necessary purchase. This distraction is slowly tearing us away from practical and useful experiences, such as family time, nights out with friends, the ability to sit, think, read, or be creative.

Technology has seeped in and taken over almost every aspect of our lives, consuming our time and space, and we have never been strategic about understanding its true cost. All we know is we're overloaded and don't know what to do. We have been backed into a corner and do not know how to get back out.

Just think about all the plugs you need for the varying devices in life. It's crazy! I believe when I was a teenager we could have gotten by with one plug in our living room for the television and maybe a lamp. That was it.

Now I need a plug for my phone, laptop, kids' phones, Bluetooth speakers, headsets, monitors, and so on. The amount of cords our family has to pack to go on vacation is ridiculous. I look into my bag, thinking we packed a giant spider because of the thick white web laid at the bottom of the suitcase.

The overall result from this type of living is an extremely distracted culture always looking for the next fix. We have lost the concept of delayed gratification. Our children, many of whom are now adults having grown up in this culture, no longer know how to be bored and the creative aspects that can come from such an experience.

We're losing relationship skills as we become more narcissistic; losing important cognitive thinking skills, such as critical analytic thinking; and let's not forget about FOMO (Fear of Missing Out). Many people may not even finish this book because they're too distracted and want to move on to another venture.

This isn't even discussing how many people are neglecting their bodies, health, mind, and soul due to the time spent in front of some type of screen.

If we don't turn the tides in some way, we are trending toward becoming a more detached culture than ever. The issue is clear—this is a runaway train we're on, which cannot be stopped as a whole, because technology isn't going to go away. But through individual efforts, we can make a change, which is why it's important for us to understand our own relationship with technology.

Confused Culture

There are issues, messages, and thoughts plaguing our culture and causing increased, and mainly hidden, confusion. Now, this section is not meant to be politically correct, nor address these issues. The main point is to show how movements such as extreme feminism, misguided masculinity, lack of direction, poor parenting, deteriorating values, racial tension, entitlement, or protests cause significant impact in our culture. But without clear understanding of the purpose and aim of these movements, we're compounding confusion in our lives.

No matter where you stand on these subjects, there's an underlying impact being placed upon individuals because of these movements. The end result is usually wrapped up in confusion on what to think or how to act, and this eventually evolves into stress. At times, this stress becomes apparent without the individual even realizing the effects, which is evident in the angry outbursts happening at protests and "peaceful" demonstrations.

The confusion begins to unravel when young men do not know how to treat women due to societal or ultra-feminist expectations. Both young men, women, and eventually families are hurt by the confusion. When young mothers are chided for breastfeeding or choosing a bottle, or for homeschooling versus going to public school; chastised for staying at home or pursuing a career. The unrealistic pressure puts ridiculous and unnecessary stress upon the entire family.

The NFL players taking a knee or sitting during the anthem is another recent example of confusion and stress being added into the mix. A sport which was usually reserved for entertainment and escape entered the political landscape. Confusion began to arise in the locker rooms as entire teams stayed in the tunnel during the anthem to avoid putting added stress on the players, or make them feel "uncomfortable" in deciding what stance they should take during the anthem. A usually rote practice became surrounded in controversy and confusion with players, owners, coaches, and fans all attempting to understand how to respond.

When we lose the freedom of speech—except speech deemed acceptable by certain groups—confusion arises over what to say, or even how to express our own thoughts or opinions due to fear of retaliation or isolation by other groups. When young people are violently protesting against movements they don't entirely understand, anger and hatred begin to swell up in their lives, and they cannot completely explain nor fully comprehend how to deal with it appropriately.

The University of California, Berkley, the birthplace of free speech, has recently had five violent outbursts on campus in response to the topic of free speech.

The problem is real. Fists are flying at peace rallies. Violence and fights are breaking out in the "empathy tents," which are supposed to be safe places for protesters to unwind and relax during the rally. The art of civilized conversation is slowly being eroded and replaced by the loudest voice.

In our quest for "equality," we have snubbed age-old cultures and traditions simply because they're not in line with certain modern standards. In essence, we have thrown the baby out with the bath water. What we have is an entire generation that doesn't know how to properly relate, speak, communicate, be sympathetic, or even understand that it is all right to disagree. All they are left with is confusion and a grossly distorted view of self. Confusion can then erode faith and hope, resulting in "Self" becoming the sole entity to be worshipped.

When Self is worshipped, then anything contrary to its entitled rights is offensive. And somehow, "being offended" has become an inalienable right. This is very wrong.

When you make life about you and your pursuits, you're automatically exclusionary. Especially in a culture which will berate, demean, and even result in violence against those people who do not share their common thinking.

This is the result of the problem when you only stand for Self. It's a very narrow walkway enmeshed in confusion, and it can be influenced by many different causes.

We don't know what to stand for anymore because we are condemned when we do stand for our beliefs. The confusion keeps mounting as people keep searching for some type of foundation. At a basic level they're attempting to understand their own identity. With so many slippery foundations placed before people, it has become increasingly difficult to know where to stand without being knocked down.

You need to be cognizant of this general confusion in our culture and how it is affecting your own life. You must recognize that you live in a turbulent culture tossing with each wave, searching for some place to land. The need to understand your own identity apart from this confusion is important in creating a solid foundation to live a truly Thrival Life.

I Did It My Way!

Another side effect of our culture confusion is that it will leave an individual self-absorbed. When we don't know how to properly relate to culture, our natural inclination is to only look to one's Self. To protect Self, do what is best for Self, and promote Self at all costs.

Unfortunately, the end result is people become greedy, selfish, and self-absorbed. A self-absorbed individual is not one who thrives. By virtue, all they're doing is attempting to survive—to knock down or knock out anyone who doesn't agree with them or see them as important as they do themselves. We see this manifest itself in various ways throughout our culture, from entitled individuals to angry and violent protesters, and to the lack of care for our neighbors.

Whether we admit it or not, we have a very materialistic outlook on life. We judge and are judged by how much we own and can accumulate. We eschew difficult situations and seek only ease and comfort in our pursuits of careers, relationships, and circumstances. Addictions are on the rise as we cannot get enough of our desires, cravings, and ambitions to cover the hole in which this way of thinking leaves us.

We must tread carefully when experimenting with various substances, because once we indulge in them, it becomes easier to jump into whatever vice is available with both feet. This lack of discipline spills over and exposes itself in our lack of compassion for others. The idea of serving others is lost because selfishness only puts ourselves first.

A self-centered culture will eventually lead to seeking personal comfort, material possessions, and a do-anything-at-any-cost attitude. People who are living this kind of lifestyle are confused as to why there's a hole in their lives, and they will use any numbing device to curtail their pain. Those on the other side are riddled with confusion because they don't know if they should be joining into the party or not. Either way, the stress and worry is continually escalating because of a complete lack of looking beyond Self.

This viewpoint manifests itself in having an individualistic view of progress, society, and success instead of a communal attitude. A true communal attitude puts the community above Self in the quest for a thriving life.

I Don't Need Help

The secondary result of a self-absorbed culture is the thought that "I am a self-made individual and do not need anyone's help." Once this thinking becomes commonplace, then the need for relationships becomes unnecessary.

We're already seeing this problem manifest itself in different ways throughout culture. For instance, we don't know how to interact appropriately with others anymore, using social media or email as a shield when having difficult conversations.

Until recently, these types of conversations have always required a face-to-face meeting, but social media has raised a generation of people unable to connect properly with one another. There's a lack of comprehension over how our words can hurt someone online. This is because the screen acts as a filter so we're not speaking directly in their face.

Christopher Bergland, a researcher from the University of Vermont, discussed our need for face-to-face conversations. He stated, "The latest scientific research shows that making eye contact and interpreting eye movements is paramount to forming strong social bonds. Looking someone directly in the eyes at some point during a conversation is the key to making any social, professional, or deep romantic connection. All of us rely on eye contact to communicate and connect with one another on an intellectual and emotional level."

By spending all our time on social media and using technology to have these conversations, we're missing out on the effects these interactions could have on the other person. For instance, when you're delivering challenging news, you miss out on crucial social cues because you can't look the recipient in the eyes. You also can't see their immediate physical response, thereby resulting in a lack of empathy because you're removed from the situation.

This is why I have repeatedly told my boys they can never break up with a girl through the use of any type of technology. If they're going to break a girl's heart, then they need to do it in a face-to-face manner. They need to understand the importance of the pain the conversation may cause the other person, no matter how uncomfortable the moment is for them. These conversations should never be easy, because we should never have a heart so cold where the heartache is simply another cold message sent in the quiet comfort of technology.

We're becoming more and more detached—creating self-made individuals whose only purpose is the promotion of Self. Without the understanding or thinking that we have the need to reach out and ask for help, we are limiting our comprehension of alternative methods, ideas, or processes to make our lives better.

Vice Admiral Vivek Murthy, the 19th Surgeon General of the United States, writes how this condition is making us lonelier than ever, especially in the workplace. This epidemic is causing a lasting effect on our lives, health, and relationships. Vivek states, "Loneliness and weak social connections are associated with a reduction in lifespan similar to that caused by smoking 15 cigarettes a day and even greater than that associated with obesity. Loneliness is also associated with a greater risk of cardiovascular disease, dementia, depression, and anxiety. At work, loneliness reduces task performance, limits creativity, and impairs other aspects of executive function such as reasoning and decision making."

This detachment is growing and causing people to not have any idea how to properly interact with each other. Think about how this lack of communication will impact marriages, parenting, teaching, business, and community. If we don't ever learn to reach out for healthy help, we have imprisoned ourselves to live lives in the limits of our own experiences.

The purpose of the Thrival Life is to engage others and get back on a recognizable trail for a common good. To stop living for Self and create an existence which is thriving regardless of the circumstances surrounding us.

4

LACK OF PREPARATION

Unprepared for Modern Living

"By failing to prepare, you are preparing to fail."
~ Benjamin Franklin

I will admit I'm not the best at preparation. I don't know if it's an adventurous spirit or a lazy attitude which contributes to this derivation of my psyche. The outcome is that on more than one occasion, I have not packed properly for a trip or vacation.

Part of what plays into this mindset is I have travelled extensively for work. In those times it became second nature to know what to pack and what I needed. I became so good that if it was only a one-night trip, I could get all I needed packed into my laptop bag. The repetitiveness and experience of business travel has probably given me a false sense of security when it comes to being prepared in other areas of my life.

I was extremely grateful last summer when Anna and Rachel offered to pack my backpack for a hike with our Knights of Heroes girls. We were heading out on a two-day trip into the Pike National Forest. While I have hiked and camped extensively, I had never backpacked over several days. If left to my own devices, I could have easily packed what I thought was needed. But then I would have soon realized my pack was too heavy, and I would have been starving.

To complicate issues, on the night we were packing, I was pulled away to address an issue at the boys' camp. This was when Anna and Rachel came in with their magical backpacking powers. Anna is like the Mary Poppins of backpacking. The number of items she can pull out of her seemingly small backpack is nothing short of wondrous.

Anna and Rachel packed the right cooking equipment, all the food that was necessary, my bedroll, and the necessities we don't speak about in the woods. My backpack was a vision of beauty. Their preparation was amazing, not just for me, but for the rest of the group heading out into the woods.

This experience was somewhat reminiscent of how I spend a lot of time in my life. Instead of preparing properly or being humble enough to ask the people who know how to prepare properly, I attempt to make it all on my own. While this attitude might work in certain parts of my life, a lack of preparation does not work well for life itself.

The bottom line for our society is we are ill-prepared to live in our modern world. For thousands of years, our way of living was the same from generation to generation. In today's world, even in the same generation, there can be multiple iterations of technology, thought, politics, or basic living. We're not prepared to live a fully adaptable life when we need to carefully inspect anything new which comes our way and interpret how it will fit into our lives.

As quickly as culture, spirituality, philosophy, and thought have changed, we have made very little effort to adjust our lives to live properly or even live abundantly within the midst of these rapid changes. We have sat idly by and let others tell us how to live, without uttering a word. The passive stance has affected our ability to adapt and be responsible—because we don't have to grow up, do we?

Lost Art of Adulting

Remember the times when you were just an adult, and it was a naturally occurring event which happened with age and maturity? Not something you aspired to be only when it was convenient, or some great accomplishment in life.

Unfortunately, nowadays we have made being an adult a verb, something you do on occasion when you feel like it, instead of a defining noun of who you are. We have made *adulting* a term that garners laughter—we have it emblazoned on t-shirts, coffee mugs, and memes.

When we make being an adult a choice, it usually ends with mixed consequences. Because we have made this natural progression in life somewhat optional, we skipped steps that would have otherwise properly prepared us to live a more thriving life.

This lack of acceptance of our own responsibility, or the lack of personal accountability, is being manifested in negative behaviors such as immaturity, disrespect, entitlement, increased selfishness, and extreme negativity, which serve as poor examples for the next generation.

This, in turn, prevents individuals from maturing and progressing in a natural manner, and consequently accepting the next stages in life appropriately. Without this proper foundation, how can anyone adequately prepare for all the challenges of this modern age?

Our movement from childhood, teenage years, young adult, and into adulthood is a natural progression where growth and maturity should be happening at each stage to prepare us for the next. For thousands of years, young people completed communal rites of passage through ceremonies to symbolize their transition from one stage of life to the next.

You knew from an early age what would be expected of you at each level. When you reached a particular age, either through an individual rite of passage with family or with the community, you left the old ways of thinking and living behind, and moved forward onto the next stage.

The pathway to become a Knight is one of the greatest examples of the rites of passage. You began the journey as a Page cleaning the stables and caring for the Knights' horses. Once you completed your assigned tasks and training as a Page, you would become a Squire. As a Squire, you would begin to learn the art of sword fighting, riding a horse, and the gentlemanly aspects of becoming a Knight. Only when you have fulfilled all the requirements of a Squire would you be knighted.

You became a Knight because you had a specific role, with well-defined expectations, to fulfill in protecting and contributing back into the community. The community needed you to make the jump in order to contribute to the well-being of everyone. There wasn't much use for a lifelong Page in society.

In our modern times, without this natural progression, we are in no way prepared for the next stage in life because we never mastered our current circumstances. Now we don't know how to act or know what's expected of us when moving onto another stage.

These stages of life have become melded together. There's no longer a distinct line of crossing from one stage of childhood to youth and onto adulthood. What we end up with is more pressure and stress to perform and be better in every stage, instead of being able to master the pressure and deal with it in context.

Young people are accepting far more responsibility than they're capable of handling. While they may have been well-trained in a certain task, like creating apps or software, they're in no way prepared to run their own company to sell the app. The end result is that they are becoming increasingly overwhelmed at an alarming rate. They have the knowledge, but have not been trained to deal with the stress and pressures that may come along with the responsibilities they have assumed.

We have to be able to prepare ourselves properly in each stage of life. Then make a specific and defined progression to the next stage. This allows us not to adult when we feel like it, but be an adult, because this is who we are and the responsibilities we have accepted in our lives for the greater good of our families and community.

A Lasting Effect

Our inability to accept our future transfers over to those individuals we're raising who feel they're only responsible when it's convenient for them. This causes people to look in all the wrong places for happiness, joy, and contentment in life.

We're losing the important aspect of modeling what a happy, well-adjusted adult can look like. So why would the next generation want to "grow up" if they can continue to live like a child? A child wants everything they can have and have it now, even if it's not good for them. This is why they need to be under "adult" supervision. This is what maturity brings in—making grown-up decisions which may not be fun, but are the correct choice in the long run.

There's the fear that we would eventually lose the wise sages who disperse wisdom to the younger generation. Those men and women of great character and wisdom for which you are naturally drawn to and desire to mimic their life. If you think about it now, you can probably only name a handful of individuals who truly modeled a life you wanted to emulate.

As our culture continues to progress in this manner, we'll eventually run out of those individuals who can truly teach and prepare us for the next stage. Or worse, we ignore their advice as too antiquated or too old-fashioned for the life we think we want to live.

If we truly think this problem is going to get any better on its own, we're sadly mistaken. Without a purposeful and intentional effort on our part, this lackadaisical attitude will only get worse with each generation and evolution in technology and attitude. We need to begin to be more intentional about not only living our lives in the present, but what we want them to be in the future and for future generations.

Preparedness

If you were attempting a week-long hike or adventure, you would prepare yourself as much as possible—which I can fully comprehend now that I have gone through my own backpacking trip. You want to find the best route, ensure you have the right gear, and schedule out meals in order to have enough food. But you also can't take too much of anything since you'll have to carry the extra weight.

The irony is in how much we prepare for the activities in life, but not FOR life. We prepare for our careers by going to college, trade school, or take some specialized training. We prepare for marriage by seeking pre-marital counseling. Finances are prepared by taking budgeting courses. We take courses to write, speak, cook, hunt, work on our cars, decorate our homes, or train our kids in sports. Yet the single most important aspect of all these parts of our lives is life itself. We neglect to prepare for the central core of our being; instead, we just live and hope to survive.

We must prepare our hearts, souls, and minds better to live in this modern age appropriately. To truly learn what it means to thrive in our own lives and live a life of prosperity and mutual agreement. Without our ability to prepare, we're simply running through the forest doing the best we can with whatever we happen to come across along the way.

If I had packed my own backpack in isolation, I would've had to rely heavily on Anna and Rachel for support and food. The burden I would have placed on them would have been unfair and unnecessary, since they did prepare properly. We need to take responsibility to force our lives to turn in a positive direction.

Most of us are just surviving in this life. We survive because we have never prepared ourselves for the onslaught of hardships this life offers. How do we become happy, content, or joyful? How can we be more positive? How can we live the kind of life we'd be proud of at the end? These questions can be answered by preparing properly to live the Thrival Life.

PART 2

CULTIVATING A SURVIVAL LIFE

5

SIDE EFFECTS

What Happens When We Cultivate a Survival Life?

"While it may seem small, the ripple effect of small things is extraordinary." ~ Matt Bevin

A few years back I was training for the Triple-Bypass Cycling Race in Colorado. This is a 120-mile bike race traveling over three major mountain passes all above 10,000 feet. To get ready for the race, I was going out and riding every free afternoon. For a while, the training was great. I was getting in awesome shape. I was knocking time off my rides and progressively getting faster and more comfortable in the saddle.

The problem began to arise out of my inability to pay attention to my body. The hours and miles I was putting on my bike were beginning to cause pain in my hip. Unbeknownst to me, my hip was at the early stages of finally giving out. The excess grinding I was putting on it by cycling was causing it to deteriorate at an accelerated rate.

I had to make a choice. I was either going to simply ride the race and hope I finished, or I needed to back out of the race. I eventually rescinded my registration from the race because I didn't want to just survive the bike ride. I was also about to enter a stage in my life where I was truly going to have to navigate my hip replacement, which I had not prepared for properly.

When we don't prepare to thrive, then all we're doing is cultivating a life in survival mode. This survival mode is taking its toll on our lives. Cultivating a survival mode life is like taking swimming lessons just to keep your head above water and not drown. Training to thrive is like learning to swim because you want to dive in the Great Barrier Reef and experience all the wonder and beauty under the water.

The evolution of modern problems has produced a litany of modern side effects. Most of which result in you attempting to survive life. Whether you think you are affected by these problems or not can only be discovered as you come to understand the effects these issues have on your life.

Emotional Side Effects

A major side effect in cultivating life in survival mode is the emotional toll it takes on our lives. We're becoming more and more emotionally unstable. We're more stressed out, anxious, depressed, and confused than any other time in history. This emotional rollercoaster leads to poor self-esteem, increased mental illness, and increased substance abuse, which then results in panic attacks because people don't understand what is causing this disruption. We have become blind to the emotional side effects the stress of life is having on us.

Survival mode is crushing our emotional state. Beyond prescribing medication to simply numb us to its effects, very little is being done to look at our lives as a whole to discover how survival mode is directly affecting our emotional well-being.

Stress

The most recognizable emotional side effect is the rising levels of stress we're experiencing. According to a litany of recent research, we are more stressed than ever before.

1. **75% of adults** reported experiencing moderate to high levels of stress in the past month and nearly half reported that their stress has increased in the past year. (*American Psychological Association*)

2. Approximately **1 out of 75** people may experience panic disorder before reaching adulthood. (*National Institute of Mental Health*)

3. Stress is a top health concern for U.S. teens between 9th and 12th grade; psychologists say that if they don't learn healthy ways to manage stress now, it could have serious long-term health implications. (*American Psychological Association*)

4. 80% of workers feel stress on the job and nearly half say they need help in learning how to manage stress. And 42% say their co-workers need such help. (*American Institute of Stress*)

These statistics keep piling up every year. You probably feel stressed right now over some circumstance in your life. You also know someone who is beyond stressed because of their job or life circumstances. And in both cases, there's a feeling of helplessness in how to deal with the stress.

We live under the impression that everyone is stressed, which is true, so then what's the big deal? We're all surviving life, so why not just keep everything locked down and get by? This excuse is only adding more stress into our lives.

Anxiety

Another emotional side effect is the rising levels of anxiety. Extended stress will eventually lead to anxiety. Or we suffer from anxiety because of some stress we survived but are afraid to experience again. Author Bob Beaudine states, "Anxiety occurs when you believe your nightmares instead of your dreams." Unfortunately, when we cultivate life in survival mode, we do believe more in our nightmares than our dreams.

Author and columnist Maura Kelly observed "The United States has transformed into the planet's undisputed worry champion, so we're more anxious than anything else—and also more anxious than *anyone* else, beating out all other nations in our race to the top of the nerve-racked list. According to a recent World Health Organization study, 31 percent of Americans are likely to suffer from an anxiety problem at some point during their lifetimes."

In the pursuit to always be first, Americans have taken anxiety to a whole new level—a circumstance you need to be highly aware of in your own life. For anxiety is rarely recognized until you are completely overwhelmed and barely keeping your head above water.

Depression

In cultivating a survival life, our stress and anxiety will undoubtedly and eventually evolve into depression.

Statistics show that diagnoses of depression are growing at an alarming rate. In addition, states with higher rates of depression also show high rates of other negative health outcomes, such as obesity, heart disease, and stroke. Individuals suffering from depression are more likely to be unemployed or recently divorced than their non-depressed counterparts, and women experience greater risk of depression than men.

Depression will affect 1 in 10 Americans at some point in their lives, 80% of whom will never seek out any type of treatment. Depression is also the leading cause of disability in the United States among people aged 15 to 44. Depression ranks among the top three workplace problems in the United States along with family issues and, of course, stress.

Depression is a serious and growing issue in our culture. With problems compounding upon individuals from every angle, it's becoming increasingly difficult to manage life in an appropriate manner.

These examples are a baseline everyone can identify with on some level. Our modern problems are causing some type of angst, worry, stress, anxiety, depression, or concern in our lives in some form. But it doesn't end there.

Relationship Side Effects

Beyond the emotional side effects that we deal with daily—stress, anxiety, and depression are all having an effect on our relationships. When we are stressed and anxious, these emotions roll over into our relationships and affect every meaningful connection—from our spouses, parents, children, friends, and neighbors. This mixture of emotions also affects our relationships at work. With bosses, employees, and co-workers all feeling the brunt of people with short fuses who have become very tightly wound.

One study that followed eighty couples over four years found that those who experienced more stress outside of their relationships reported feeling less comfortable and less close with their partner. They also felt less sure of the relationship than folks who experienced less stress.

Stress can manifest itself in your relationships through irritability, lack of communication, spending more time on your phone or video games than face-to-face conversations. When we don't know how to deal with our own stresses, then we struggle to even attempt communicating the problem or inviting others in to understand the problem.

This is happening to our culture as a whole. The more we turn inward and create a cocoon around our lives in an attempt to survive life, the less likely we are to reach out and connect with others.

This causes us to miss an important part of our own growth and having someone besides ourselves to turn to when we go through difficult times. At our core level, we were built to belong in a community. When we push others away during the times we need them most, we're missing out on one of the greatest ways to achieve a Thrival Life.

Physical Side Effects

When stress, anxiety, and depression begin to unravel in our lives, there are many lasting physical side effects causing harm. We sometimes let these issues manifest themselves to the point where we have panic attacks, sleepless nights, and fatigue while losing sight of how to function on a basic level.

Historically, stress was a way to protect yourself from predators or threats that roamed around. When faced with a certain danger, "the body kicks into gear, flooding the body with hormones that elevate your heart rate, increase your blood pressure, boost your energy, and prepare you to deal with the problem." Stress was your body's way of notifying you to find a creative solution to the problem before you.

In these modern times, however, we're not usually facing life-or-death situations due to predators and threats. When our brain sends distress signals because of the day-to-day stresses we experience, our body becomes "stuck," trying to decipher and send the appropriate fight or flight responses.

We have turned traffic, news, politics, and our jobs into stressful situations, and our bodies are attempting to deal with them properly. Unfortunately, we usually don't have a solution to these problems because the solutions are beyond our control and they're not as life-threatening as our ancestral circumstances.

As a result, our bodies are declining in health. The longer we stay "stuck" in the stress cycle, the more our overall health decreases—we become overweight, we suffer from chronic high blood pressure, become at risk for heart attacks, and would probably give anything for a good night's sleep.

These issues are mainly due to your body responding to stress with headaches, muscle tension, chest pain, fatigue, change in sex drive, upset stomach, or sleeping problems. They can also cause a rise in overeating, angry outbursts, alcohol consumption, and drug and tobacco use—all of which have a direct effect on your body, on how you deal with others and the circumstances in your life.

The ongoing rise of stress in our culture is palpable and is affecting almost everyone in some form or another.

- 43% of all adults suffer adverse health effects from stress.

- About 3.4% of the U.S. population suffers from serious psychological distress.

- 75% to 90% of all doctor's office visits are for stress-related ailments and complaints.

- Stress can play a part in problems such as headaches, high blood pressure, heart problems, diabetes, skin conditions, asthma, arthritis, depression, and anxiety.

- Around one-third of adults reported experiencing feeling nervous or anxious (36%), irritability or anger (35%), and fatigue (34%) due to their stress in the past year.

You can probably identify with the tense nature your body has developed. From tight shoulders and back to frequent headaches, these are all in response to your body's attempt to "deal" with the stress in your life.

The longer we live within this "stuck" state, the greater toll it takes on our body and mind. We have to learn the basics of living and eliminating stress in our lives, or else our lives with be short-lived.

Mental Side Effects

We also need to understand the mental side effects all the stress and anxiety are causing. Since we are so distracted, stressed out, and fretting about our lives, our thoughts become erratic. Our minds are disjointed, and we lack clarity in understanding in which direction we should progress.

In order to deal with our stress and anxiety, we take medication at an alarming rate. We need a prescription to sleep, to think, to wake up, and to function in some cases. Our Red Bull society lives in a constant state of being overwhelmed, which prevents us from seeing clearly the way forward.

The larger issue with this mental instability is that we're missing out on our meaningful work. We're either too distracted or cannot concentrate on the one thing that gives us purpose, meaning, and a healthy pursuit.

This is probably our greatest miss. Mainly because if we could get our focus on something important, something that has brought life to our souls, we could better deal with many of the issues in our lives. We could find purpose and begin to unravel ourselves from the web we have been caught in.

Gross Reality

Now, I'm not trying to be the grim reaper here—I simply want to paint a picture of living in this modern world. We are carrying around a larger burden on our shoulders than we realize. The pressures, anxieties, concerns, and changes are greater than any other time in history, and it is having an effect on our lives. Yet, we are rarely shown how to adapt, or live effectively, within these rapid changes.

We're essentially living our lives in these contained balloons, doing the best we can. There's nothing wrong with this, except this is really our only survival mechanism. But every time a new technology, problem, issue, process, or revelation comes along, we're just adding more air into the balloon. The balloon keeps expanding and we don't know what to do with it until a certain time when it pops. Usually in some catastrophic event.

Most of our reactions to this life are self-induced and our responses are usually within our control. But the problem exacerbates when the external issues are flying at us so quickly and with such force and volume, we get caught in a cycle of not being able to process the externals properly in order to reverse them.

No matter your background—teacher, mom, dad, preacher, CEO, stay-at-home parent, executive, or mailroom clerk, these issues affect your life in some way. These problems are also affecting the people you are dealing and interacting with on a daily basis. Individuals who are consumed by stress and unable to get unstuck.

The state of cultivating a survival life explains why people blow up in the grocery store and raise their middle finger in traffic. The rise of fighting inside fast food restaurants or people yelling at the cashier in McDonald's for taking too long with their order. We're so tightly wound up that the smallest, most insignificant road bumps can send us over the edge.

These are the burdens and problems all of us are facing. Some people deal with the issues and burdens better than others. The majority of us have simply learned how to live with the confusion because we don't want to admit we may not know what is happening.

For the most part, we simply don't know what to do. We have been stuck in the wilderness making the best way we know how and going to bed exhausted each night because no one has shown us how to stop cultivating life in survival mode and trained us in how to thrive. If we don't stop and make a drastic change, then we'll truly be living the majority of our lives in survival mode and our side effects will only worsen.

6

SURVIVAL MODE

What Happens When You Live in Survival Mode?

"In a mad world, only the mad are sane."
~ **Akira Kurosawa**

Although we were blessed with three children in less than three years—to say we were in survival mode is an understatement! I only vaguely remember this fog of diapers, baby powder, bottles, and baby food swirling around the house.

I was attempting to work my job, and my wife was adjusting to this new lifestyle with three toddlers running around the house, usually at full speed, buck naked, and screaming at the top of their lungs. The circumstances created quite a chaotic time in our lives. To top it off, we were selling our house and moving to Colorado to begin a new adventure.

This was a new stage in our lives, and nothing, or no one, could have probably prepared us for what we were going to experience. The only solace I had was in knowing Joseph, a colleague with an 18-month-old and whose wife had just given birth to triplets. I would often find Joseph at his desk with his hands on the keyboard, staring blankly at the screen. He wasn't typing anything—I think the office was the only place he could find quiet.

Joseph would go on in this panicked, semi-catatonic state to explain the amount of formula and diapers he would have to buy at Costco. And the schedule they had to keep in order to ensure everyone was fed the same. Joseph and his wife were truly living in survival mode, trying to figure out this new stage of life.

When you enter these stages of life, you become overwhelmed because they are new. No amount of reading or instruction could probably prepare you for this stage because you really can't understand what it's like until you're completely immersed in its reality.

Survival Mode

On our way to live a Thrival Life, we may find ourselves having to live in survival mode for short periods of time while learning to adjust to new circumstances—and that's all right. The problem occurs when we never learn to make the proper adjustments to move out of survival mode.

When we begin to unravel the stress, anxiety, pressures, and expectations that are coming at us from every direction, we begin to see how easily we can live in survival mode. When the amount of pressures and expectations are exponentially rising, balanced against very little instruction on how to handle them appropriately in our lives, we succumb to simply surviving life.

The circumstances are really no one's fault. We are truly trying to do our best, but the number of stresses and expectations placed upon us are grossly out-weighed by any proper instruction given to us to live an authentic Thrival Life.

This is our reality. It's the reason why we have been living in survival mode. We're simply trying to keep our heads above water in order to avoid getting too over-whelmed. Unfortunately, this model doesn't work very well for anyone in the long term.

Survival mode can be fine for a time—a shelter you enter to weather a storm or get past a rough spot. But it's not a place to live life. When you stay in this spot for extended periods, the tension it creates in your life has to give at some point.

You'll finally get to a breaking point and seek out an alternative solution. Unfortunately, there are usu-ally only two solutions to choose in survival mode. You either attempt to distract yourself from your pain and misery, or you become fully destructive with your life.

Distractive Solutions

When faced with a life in survival mode, you'll soon need to distract yourself from this constant pain. Whether this is a conscious or unconscious decision can depend upon how long you have been in a place of survival.

On a very basic level, you know this is not a place in which you belong. The situation is uncomfortable and something does not sit well. You don't know how to get out of this stuck position to deal with the problems, handle the stress in your life, or face your fears so you can move forward. Instead, you attempt to numb yourself from the pain, which temporarily takes away the negative emotions associated with your stress or fears.

But because this is only a temporary solution, the end result can lead to destructive consequences. The rise in alcohol and drug addictions, and prescription drug abuse to name a few. While we can justify our use of such substances in social instances, we need to understand the reason we're abusing them to relieve stress in order to unveil the real issue.

A recreational drink usually reserved for social settings suddenly becomes an activity done nightly in private. We just want to stop the pain and thoughts running through our head in order to get a couple hours of sleep.

The prescription Vicodin you were prescribed for a knee surgery last year suddenly becomes a nightly ritual. Or having to take Advil PM to get some sleep at night—followed by a full pot of black coffee to wake you up in the morning.

When reviewing alcohol statistics, use has risen dramatically over the past few years in the United States. In fact, the Journal of the American Medical Association stated "High-risk and problem drinking increased far more dramatically. High-risk drinking, in this study, referred to women drinking four or more drinks in a day, or men drinking five or more drinks in a day, on a weekly basis. High-risk drinking overall rose by 29.9 %."

Problems with alcohol increased by nearly 50%. Among women, alcohol abuse and dependence increased by 83.7%. Among black people, it increased by 92.8%. Among the poor (earning less than $20,000) it rose by 65.9%.

Prescription drug use has been on the rise with roughly 60% of Americans on some type of prescribed medication.

While the reasons people are drinking more, doing more drugs, and on prescription medication can vary, the need to numb the pain, relax, or calm down are the norms.

Researchers are calling this a "public health crisis." The stress of living in our modern times is literally becoming unbearable. Income and educational disparities, as well as "unemployment, residential segregation, discrimination, decreased access to health care, and increased stigma associated with drinking," may also play a role.

We're literally not comfortable enough in our own skin when it comes to our jobs, income, or overall roles in society. Thus we need to find some mechanism to numb our pain.

This is survival mode at its best. You'll keep pushing through the pain and misery of the life you're living as long as you have some way to numb your pain at the end of the day. Substance use or abuse then becomes your survival mechanism—the way you deal with the stresses and anxiety delivered through this modern life.

Destructive Solutions

When the use of drugs or alcohol are not enough to help some people deal with their current circumstances, they'll move on to more drastic measures. For many young people, they resort to cutting, self-harm, and suicide. These measures are all on the rise as young people are seeking some solution to deal with the stress and problems in their lives.

A study by the NHS showed "The sharp upward trend in under-18s being admitted to hospitals after poisoning, cutting or hanging themselves is more pronounced among girls, though there have been major rises among boys too." Experts say the rise is a shocking confirmation that more young people are experiencing serious psychological distress because they are under unprecedented social pressures. Self-harm and cutting are ways for these teens to either numb the pain or feel a different pain besides their current misery.

For other people, it still gets worse. When the drugs, alcohol, or self-harm are not enough, they turn to suicide as an alternative solution. At children's hospitals, admissions of patients 5 to 17 years old for such thoughts or actions more than doubled from 2008 to 2015. About 121 people take their lives every day and some 44,000 commit suicide each year.

In less than 10 years the suicide rate has doubled among young people due to stress from school, pressure from parents, pressure from social media, and access to multiple ways to commit suicide on the Internet. Young people are believing an incredible lie about the value of their lives and how to solve their problems.

This phenomenon is being brought to light by the suicides of such famous rock stars as Chris Cornell of Soundgarden and Chester Bennington of Linkin Park. Both took their own lives within a short time period of each other in 2017.

Suicide has become an increasingly used alternative to seeking help or pushing through a problem. Living in survival mode with no access to the correct coping tools, we have let our children and society down.

We need to be more vocal about the alternatives out there. There truly is a thriving life where you can live an awesome life beyond your wildest dreams. But it's going to take time and effort to get to that place.

We need to stop cultivating life in survival mode and using alternative modes to numb our pain. Because there is a better way to live, in pursuit of the Thrival Life.

PART 3

TRAINING TO THRIVE
PREPARING FOR MODERN-DAY LIFE

7

CREATING A BETTER JOURNEY

Building a Solid Foundation

"I always thought that the 'thriving' would come when everything was perfect, and what I learned is that it's actually down in the mess that things get good." ~ Joanna Gaines

One day, you decide to run a marathon. Now, logic would hold that if you wanted to successfully complete the marathon, you would need to train. You would find a good exercise routine that could slowly help you increase your endurance. A good diet, cross-training, and stretching regime would be added in to strengthen your muscles and reduce body ache. You would then rearrange your schedule to make the marathon a priority and keep yourself from being distracted by other activities.

If you were serious, you wouldn't sit around and do nothing. Or even worse, your "training" would involve practice runs of dialing 911. Practice learning how to insert an IV in your arm for rehydration. You could even rehearse how to collapse gracefully along the marathon route, just in case a video of your fall was uploaded to the Internet.

If you choose to run a marathon, you're more likely training to finish the race with your arms above your head, instead of simply surviving the race and being glad it is over.

In order to live a better life, we need to stop cultivating life in survival mode and begin to train to thrive. The process of thriving entails eliminating distractions and being intentional about living a more impactful life. The purpose of the Thrival Life is to live a better journey, not just survive along the trail. The desire is to live your own Thrival Adventure so you're not living someone else's.

The Thrival Life

The Thrival Life means living life with all the fervor, passion, and intention you possess to generate maximum impact. You acknowledge there are distractions in your life, but you intentionally remove the obstacles that keep you from pursuing a life in which your dreams and desires are fulfilled. It is knowing you possess something greater inside you to give to the world—something the world desperately needs.

The Thrival Life gives you the power to reject the repeated messages which have inadvertently put you in survival mode. The stress and anxiety of living in survival mode pushes you onto a narrow path that forces limited thinking. Most of your life statements begin with "But I can't, because..." You no longer desire to live in this state of mind, so you are willing to make the necessary changes to pursue your dreams and live a passionate thriving life.

The Thrival Life is not a destination on a map but a journey you take to live a more fulfilled life. The journey pushes you into a more positive, purposeful, and wider path of opportunities and pursuits.

The pathway toward living a Thrival Life will not come easy and must be built upon a very solid foundation from where all areas of your life will flow. The first step you need to take is to create the foundation to build a solid groundwork in living your life.

This guide is meant to be used along with the Thrival Guidebook in order to give you an opportunity to sufficiently write out your thoughts and create a specific pathway for you to live a thriving life. You can download the guidebook at www.thethrivalguide.com.

Creating Your Compass

You begin the process of building your foundation by creating your own personal Compass. The Compass is the key to any adventure—it keeps you on track, guides you to your destination, and prevents you from getting lost. You keep your Compass on you at all times during any adventure in order to maintain your course and not veer off the trail.

To move toward, and maintain, the Thrival Life, you'll need to create your own personal Compass. Just like the 4 points on an actual compass, there are 4 attributes to creating your Compass.

1. **Thrival North** – Thrival North is the person you want to be or become. Not what you do in life, but the person who is behind what you do.

2. **Thrival Code** – The Thrival Code is what keeps you focused on your journey. The map to ensure you reach your destination.

3. **Thrival Adventure** – Your Thrival Adventure is the good work you are committing to in this moment of life.

4. **Thrival Charge** – The Thrival Charge is the motivation to keep you on your specific pathway. A way to avoid discouragement during challenging times.

Each point on a compass is important in finding your way. Your Compass needs to maintain each of these points as well, in order to ensure you stay on the path of the Thrival Life.

Finding Your Thrival North

Your foundation for a Thrival Life begins by finding your Thrival North. Your Thrival North is not what you want to accomplish or what you want to do, but rather what you want to be in life. The person you want to be remembered as, or aspire to, regardless of what you are doing. It is the steadfast point of your life that will not change in spite of your circumstances.

Thrival North is steadfast and constant. Geographically, navigation north, or true north, is the location of the North Pole at any given place on the planet. No matter where you are on earth, if you have a compass that is calibrated correctly, you can always find north.

For your life, you want to have a steadfast place keeping you aligned in all your decisions, circumstances, and changes—the fixed point from which the direction of your life will flow. This point is your Thrival North.

While your purpose, adventures, or passions in life might change, your Thrival North should not. This is the concrete definition of the person for whom you want to be remembered. It is a solid foundation to build on the rest of your life.

Defining Your Thrival North

Your Thrival North is not your passion, your purpose, or all those other statements no one knows how to define in their life. Rather, it's based on who you are, or maybe the person you want to become. It's the fixed point in your life where everything else can begin to grow. Think bigger and deeper around what you want to be remembered for and the type of person you want to become.

Ask yourself the following questions to discover your Thrival North:

- What do you value?
- What do you want to be known for?
- What legacy do you want to leave behind?
- What motivates you, gets you excited?
- What brings you down?
- What good things would you pursue if there were no restrictions?

Once you get a firm foundation of what your Thrival North looks like, you can begin to understand what you want to accomplish. Whether you call it your passion, purpose, or life pursuit, these may all change throughout your life due to varying circumstances, but your Thrival North should never change and should always reflect back the true person in you.

The Thrival Code

Once you begin to understand your Thrival North, you need to ensure you have a good map to guide you. The Thrival Code is the map which works with your Compass to guide you as you seek the Thrival Life. The Thrival Code helps you understand the path, identify the dangerous places in life, and gain your bearings of where you are headed.

The Knights of Heroes camp is built around the Knights Code. Every morning, we give the young men and women a part of the code. The code gives the campers the ability to live within a comprehensive foundation during the week of camp. At the end of camp, we reflect with the campers on how they have lived up to each aspect of the code.

The hope is that by the end of the week, when the campers leave the camp, they will take this code back to their homes, schools, and communities to live a life beyond the expectations of this world. A life of meaning, which will challenge them to become more than they could ever have imagined.

To live a Thrival Life, you need to attach yourself to something greater than yourself or your own story. You need specific tenets to keep you focused and not distracted. The Thrival Code is the map to guide you in living a focused Thrival Life. It is a guide to keep you from veering off the path and establish Thrival North in your own life. As you read through the guide to understand how to transform your own life, use the Thrival Code as the map to keep your journey on track.

The Thrival Code consists of seven tenets that you can constantly look back upon in order to create a thriving life. They are the guardrails to help you focus on your Thrival North, assisting you to identify those distractions that keep you in survival mode. Use the code in every choice you make—from career, family, relationships, and activities—as an overarching guide in all your pursuits.

- **Truth** – The Thrival Life practices honest and truthful actions, which bring about a well-lived life. A life devoid of truth and honesty is a life lived in survival mode.

- **Honor** – Choose to act in an honorable way in all dealings and interactions. Regardless of the outcome, you know you have behaved in a way that did not sacrifice your beliefs.

- **Respect** – In pursuing the Thrival Life, you treat others with respect, dignity, and high regard because you know you're a part of a community and need others to truly thrive.

- **Integrity** – Your life should be built around integrity. You should attach yourself to a higher cause with principles and morals. And never be afraid to put these principles into practice.

- **Valor** – You will need to be courageous in life and not be afraid of risk to achieve the life you want. Taking risks for a greater purpose will bring about more intentional results.

- **Attitude** – Maintain a positive attitude in service to others. Never let your circumstances dictate how you respond to a situation.

- **Loyalty** – Survival mode is jumping from relationship to relationship. In the Thrival Life, you will be unyielding in your loyalty to others—even if the loyalty is not reciprocated.

Go to www.thethrivalguide.com and download your free Thrival Code to display in your car, on your bathroom mirror, or office. Place the code in a visible location so you can constantly remind yourself not to settle as you strive toward the Thrival Life. You were truly made for so much more. You are choosing to live a life beyond survival mode.

Your Next Thrival Adventure

Once you begin to understand your Thrival North, it's time to start your next Thrival Adventure. Life is the culmination of the numerous mini-adventures we take, making up the whole of our own personal journey. You probably have multiple adventures in your heart, many passions or goals you want to pursue in life.

Your Thrival Adventure may be the passion that may be in your heart at this current moment. The "one good work" you want to pursue right now. Your Thrival Adventure could be caring for your kids, starting a new business, founding a nonprofit, planning for retirement, creating a conference, or serving in the community.

The importance of understanding your Thrival North is comprehending how your stress, worry, and distractions are keeping you from your next Thrival Adventure.

The purpose of the Thrival Life is not to simply quit activities or distractions, but to remove the distractions that are keeping you from doing something greater. You have to make sure your next Thrival Adventure is in line with your Thrival North, and you'll be able to achieve the overall goals of the person you want to become.

My Thrival Adventure looks different every day in order to align to my Thrival North. Some days, my Thrival Adventure is writing. Other days, it is working with the Knights of Heroes organization. Still, on different days, my Thrival Adventure is spent with my family, building my relationships with my wife and children. I also volunteer, mentor, coach, or counsel others to guide them in their own pursuit of a better life.

Your Thrival Adventure is the pursuit you are giving primary attention to at this given moment. Don't hurt yourself thinking about your own Thrival North or Thrival Adventure. Your main goal is to think about what stirs your heart. When you begin the process of finding your Thrival North, you probably know more about how to define it than you realize. You may already be involved in activities or pursuits that may be your Thrival Adventure.

As you read through this guide, begin to align your next Thrival Adventure toward a specific goal—that deep desire gnawing at you for some time to begin. Your Thrival Adventure may come easy, or you may need to spend some time thinking about what you want to pursue. Once you pinpoint your Thrival Adventure, identify what distractions in your life keep you from pursuing your next great Thrival Adventure.

If you're unable to clarify or define your own Thrival Adventure at this moment, that is fine. As you go through this guide and look at the many different distractions in your life, be cognizant of every instance you let a distraction consume your time. What are you being kept from? What could your compass be pointing you toward? What more impactful intentional activity could you have engaged in for a greater purpose instead of the distraction?

The Thrival Charge

The final process in creating your Compass is formulating your own personal Thrival Charge. The Thrival Charge is your life-giving statement that will keep you focused and determined in your journey toward the Thrival Life. Some might call it a mantra or creed to speak over your life as you engage in this monumental change. Your Thrival Charge is a statement you speak over yourself to keep you focused on your Compass.

Your transformation from living life in survival mode to a thriving life is going to be met with resistance. You might want to quit or go back, and friends and family could become major obstacles if they attempt to talk you out of your Thrival Adventure. You might want to go off course and just lie down. The negativity can become overwhelming.

But you are a fighter—you don't give up. To ensure you stay in the game, come up with your own Thrival Charge—a short phrase of encouragement you can put on your computer screen, a sticky note on your car, or write it on your mirror. It'll serve as a constant reminder that you truly do have what it takes to finish this race, and you will not be deterred in the process.

Mark Divine, a former Navy Seal turned author and motivator, calls these affirmations "power statements." They're short phrases you can repeat to yourself for encouragement, such as "you got this" or "you can do it." He says, "You will want to develop a power statement, one with some shock force to it that resonates with you. Then practice it daily."

The idea here is to inject a positive statement as encouragement for you to overcome a possible negative situation. It's the fuel you need to keep going when you're tired and ready to quit. Your Thrival Charge can build confidence in you—enough to help you take the first step necessary to be more confident in living a Thrival Life.

Creating Your Thrival Charge

When generating your own Thrival Charge, be creative. Use your imagination in a way that truly resonates with your life. You want to build confidence with your positive traits and in what you can accomplish.

Don't create something so complicated that you forget what your charge states or means. Your Thrival Charge needs to have impact and power behind it in order to keep you focused when times get tough. Your charge will help you identify your own distractions and what you need to eliminate to live a more fulfilling life.

Some examples of a Thrival Charge are:

- I am strong.
- I am fearless.
- I will not back down.

- I will not let my past define my future.

- I got this.

You can use a quote, a line from a movie, or something your father always told you. You can use a Bible verse, like my favorite scripture, which is Philippians 4:13, "I can do all things through Christ who gives me strength."

Make sure you remember the quote as something that can motivate you to keep moving forward—to never give up pursuing a life beyond your imagination.

When you create your own Thrival Charge, come up with a statement that can keep you going through the trying times. Begin by answering the following questions:

- What is your best quality?

- What keeps you going when times get tough?

- What do others say about you?

- What positive activity do you do to keep going in tough times?

- What is one thing you need to constantly remind yourself?

Now, create your own Thrival Charge, which will assist you in your pursuit of a Thrival Life. Don't let the negativity distract you in your journey. Create your charge to keep your focus and keep moving forward.

Calibrating Your Compass

Every compass needs to be calibrated. The longer you use your compass or the farther you go with it, the needle will eventually move off of true north. This is why you have to take the time to calibrate your compass every once in a while.

Your calibration could be some quick reminders of looking at your Thrival North and reminding yourself of the Thrival Code. Calibrating could be some extended time away to remind yourself of your overall journey. Even repeating your Thrival Charge to remind yourself you are strong enough to move forward might keep your focus.

Take the time to create your Compass. Remember to take it with you wherever you travel. But don't forget to constantly take the time to calibrate to ensure you're staying on track and living the Thrival Life instead of being in survival mode.

Long Game

The reason to keep going back to your Compass is because you want to play the long game. The long game is how you see success at the end of the game instead of any short-term gains.

When playing chess, you may be able to win a move here or there. But if the short strategies are the only ways you move, you'll most likely never win a game. Each move you make has to not only win the move, but more importantly, set yourself up for the next move, or three moves later. This is playing the long game.

In our "I need it now" and "get-rich-quick culture," why should you play the long game? The main reason is longevity. You want to be in your Thrival Adventure for the long haul. Short gains are simply that—short.

They won't provide you the long-term productivity you desire. Once you get one short-term gain, you are looking for another. Soon you are bouncing back and forth constantly trying to find short-term gains to satisfy your desires.

By playing the long game, as in chess, you're thinking three moves down the line. With each move and decision, you're setting yourself up for future success.

Creating the Thrival Life

The greatest plans and ideas can fail without a proper foundation to help you move forward with intention and impact. Now that you have found your Thrival North and your Thrival Code, defined your next great Thrival Adventure, and created your Thrival Charge, you have the ability to transform your own life with intention and with a far greater impact.

As you read through this guide, constantly refer back to your Compass. It is the foundational tool to help you thrive in your pursuit of the Thrival Life.

STOP SURVIVING

8

PREPARATION

Changing Your M.O.

**"The meaning of life is to find your gift.
The purpose of life is to give it away."**
~ Pablo Picasso

While serving as a church pastor for eight years, I firmly believed the role of pastor was my purpose, my Thrival North. The position was noble. It was serving and extremely satisfying. The problem was I was thinking too small in terms of my entire life. This was a huge miss on my part.

While being a pastor is noble and I did good work during my time, it was my Thrival Adventure, not my Thrival North. I was limiting a greater purpose into the confines of a role established by others.

The end result was missing out on bigger opportunities to pull my life into a more meaningful direction and being able to serve others with more intention. What I didn't see clearly then was the role of pastor was only one piece of a much larger puzzle.

Without seeing the bigger picture, I was attempting to live my life under an old paradigm. A paradigm which put each part of life into carefully constructed boxes. Unfortunately, our lives are rarely uniform, because there are far more pieces involved in the puzzle.

When I was a new pastor, social media, smart phones, and the idea of being "always on" were only starting to come to the forefront of our society. Since I had narrowly defined my role, I began to run into problems because I wasn't properly prepared for this change.

My biggest problem was my inability to handle these changes and progressions properly. Especially as an introvert, it's almost impossible for me to be "always on." I'm lucky if I'm just "dimly lit."

Years before, when I first began working in corporate America fresh out of college, none of this technology was readily available. I went to work, did my job, and then came home. My boss would only call the house in case of an extreme emergency. I could simply live my life like I always had without being constantly connected.

With the infusion of technology, there were no guides. There were no plans to tell me how to use this technology properly, how to not let it take over my life. How do I set up safe boundaries? What technology is useful and can help me, as opposed to ones that only suck my time for no purpose? When new technology came out, I simply did what a friend, the developer, or manufacturer suggested. Without any guidance, like most people, I simply let it take over my life and tried desperately to keep up.

What I needed to do was change my way of working. I needed to take control of my life, instead of letting anyone and everyone tell me how I should be living my life. I needed to be better prepared for the life I wanted to live.

A New Way of Living

In order to live more effectively in this day and age, you need a new way of thinking—a new way of living life. We have updated every part of our lives, from technology, transportation, communication, politics, and spirituality. Yet we have never figured out how to live more effectively within the construct of all of these rapid changes. To think we can keep living like we used to while constantly being introduced to new technology, ideas, and thoughts is ludicrous.

Don't get me wrong—you can definitely go off the grid and live like a caveman, which at times seems very appealing. But, if you want to live in these rapidly changing times, then you need to begin to look at life and how you do life differently. You need to learn how to be better prepared for the Thrival Adventure ahead of you.

Making Your Thrival Adventure a Priority

We have access to all this new technology but lack guidance, and this has led us to focus our attention more on recent advancements instead of our Thrival Adventure. This is where we get our priorities backwards. We mindlessly gather ideas, thoughts, technological advances and processes to create our Compass—instead of creating our Compass first and then choosing which tools will assist us in accomplishing these goals. In short, we are not preparing properly for the life we want to pursue.

Because of this, many people live a life in survival mode. They're simply attempting to keep their heads above water as they deal with their family, jobs, pursuits, and their quest for happiness. Very few truly succeed in this arena. Many people show a false view of success through social media, so we buy into the narrative and continue to think that everyone, except us, has their lives put together.

Psychologist and author Brett Steenbarger stated, "In purpose, we find energy. In energy, we find creativity, productivity, and engagement. Meaning-making makes meaningful lives. *We don't have to push ourselves to get things done when purpose pulls us toward valued outcomes.*"

This is how you can look at your Thrival North—to be pulled by your own purpose, instead of pushed by other competing priorities. Purpose is your Thrival North constantly keeping you on the right path.

Your Thrival North gives you the ability to peek above the clouds. At times, we need to have the 30,000-foot view of life. Otherwise, our heads are buried in the day-to-day tasks, which can be overwhelming, distracting, or exhausting.

There's strong science showing that having a transcendent purpose helps you change your behaviors and change your life, and at the same time, it's also good for your health. Researchers found that "people who had a weak purpose or no purpose in life were 2.4 times more likely to develop Alzheimer's disease than people who had a strong purpose in life. People with a strong purpose have been shown to live longer, to be less likely to get heart attacks and less likely to get a stroke."

If you're going to prepare yourself properly, you'll have to find your Thrival North in order to achieve your next great Thrival Adventure, and in doing so, understand your purpose and make it a priority in pursuing a Thrival Life.

Preparing for the Modern World

If we are truly honest with ourselves, we are in no way prepared to live in this modern world. We have thousands of classes, workshops, conferences, and books telling us how to do every other part of our life—except *life* itself. You can learn *tai chi*, wilderness survival, how to play the accordion, or a thousand different meditation techniques... all to help benefit you. But what about living life in general? How are we prepared to engage the most important part of life?

When you stop to think about it, life has become more complicated. The old paradigms from even 15 to 20 years ago are now extremely outdated. Society has distractions galore—from movies, the Internet, smartphones, podcasts, blogs, vlogs, Netflix, video games, Facebook, Snapchat, Twitter, sports, hobbies, reality TV, cooking shows, and so on. You have to be very intentional to be bored.

The problem is that we attempt to live the same life we've had for thousands of years among all these distractions. It simply doesn't work. But "going with the flow" is not an answer either, as you have no idea where you might land. You have to change your way of working and living to pursue something against the norm. Otherwise, you'll be swept away in the waves that are constantly crashing on the shore.

The million-dollar question now becomes: What do you do? How do you not get consumed by the waves in survival mode, but properly navigate the waters in a thriving life when there are all these problems, stressors, issues, and burdens placed upon you?

Change Your M.O.

The first step you need to take is to change your Modus Operandi, or your M.O. An M.O. is defined as a "mode of operating or working." This terminology is usually associated with police detectives. The detectives will study the patterns and thoughts of a criminal to understand motive and guess their next steps. Criminals usually get caught because the detectives figured out their way of thinking. The criminal has a specific way of doing the crime and rarely veers from the path, so detectives can predict their next step and expect the same result.

The same is true with you. If you're struggling in your life, career, relationships, or faith, and if you keep doing the same work, it will not yield different results. You need to change your M.O. Change your way of thinking and operating. This could be a simple change or it could be drastic. You need to be very creative in this place. The direction you go may be completely different than what you've anticipated, and it may also go against some ingrained beliefs you have held onto for too long.

To change your M.O., your main focus should be on remembering your Thrival North. Afterwards, you then pursue your next Thrival Adventure toward the *good work* you want to accomplish, which is the burning desire in the depths of your soul you have locked down for too long. Living a Thrival Life will take a new way of thinking, with new habits, and a shedding of distractions and clutter. You are working toward adopting a new way of living, which will help you consistently keep on track.

Own Your Journey

The second step is to own your journey. This is living your life and your Thrival Adventure instead of someone else's. No one cares more about your life than you, and no one is going to put more effort into your life than you, when it comes to igniting transformation. If you don't own your journey, then who will? If you don't live your own journey, you're more than likely working to achieve someone else's Thrival Adventure.

One Day When

One of the biggest challenges we face in pursuing our own journey is the "One Day When" lie. You say, "One day when ..." and you fill in the blank with your excuse.

One day when I get better...
One day when I have more money, or get a better job...
One day when I stop hurting...
One day when I find love or when the kids are grown...
and so on. When this magical point in time happens, then you think everything will be better and you can finally begin to chase your dreams.

This is a statement we have all made—an excuse we use to explain why we haven't pursued our own journey. The "One Day When" lie is the single greatest reason most people don't *own* their personal journeys. They're waiting for conditions and circumstances to be just right before they jump in. In reality, you need to jump in regardless of your circumstances, in order to live a thriving life.

Taking Responsibility for Your Life

Owning your journey also means you're taking responsibility for your life. Your life is yours and yours alone. No one cares more about your life and success than you. So be responsible for what happens in your life. Author and motivational speaker Farrah Gray tells you to "build your own dreams, or someone else will hire you to build theirs."

You're probably not going to win the lottery. Your job may not get better. You probably cannot count on the government. Your circumstances may never change. Transformation is up to you and you alone to ignite. And that is awesome. But this is only the first step.

You have to own it. You have to take responsibility for your own life and stop thinking it's anyone else's responsibility, or that anyone else is going to come along and save the day for you.

Optimize Your Life

The third step in owning your journey is to Optimize Your Life. This is where you analyze every aspect of your life to find out what tasks are necessary, what is moving you toward your goal, and what activities need to be eliminated. Over the last 20 to 30 years, we've had so much technology, processes, ideas, ideologies, thoughts, and ways of living pushed upon us, and we have simply let all of these updates morph into our lives. We never took the time to step back and see how a particular technology or process fits into our lives, yet we've moved forward without a proper idea or plan as to how to effectively use this new thing to our benefit.

A great example is the cell phone. We thought we needed a cell phone, so we bought one and put it in our pocket many years ago when its only function was that of a phone. All you could do was call people (crazy, I know). Then the cell phone became a smartphone, and we could do more on our phone than on a computer 20 years before. We have a world of information, and distractions, at our fingertips.

But how has it affected our lives? Is it for good or bad? Have we ever taken a step back to see how the smartphone is affecting our lives and what changes we need to make? The same can be said for the Internet, Facebook, Snapchat, Instagram, our jobs, political discussions, or religion. 200 years ago, the only concerns people had was if they had food, shelter, clothing, and whether anyone, or anything, was going to attack them. That was it. While most of us rarely think about those issues, compare that thinking to all the decisions you have to make in your life on a daily basis.

These distractions are the reason why it's so important for you to find your Thrival Adventure. You must cut through the clutter and noise of this world to find out where you specifically fit. If you were honest with yourself, you'd admit there's room to take it up a notch. The life you're living now may be comfortable, and although you desire more, you don't know how to optimize your life to get more out of what you're currently doing.

If you want to live a Thrival Life, you will optimize every aspect of life. Whether it is life in general, your career, or relationships, you will have to constantly seek ways to improve life and live with intention. Find those areas where you need to streamline and eliminate the dead weight that may be keeping you from finding your Thrival Adventure.

You optimize your life by looking at every aspect of life and making the most of what you have. You don't waste valuable time and energy on what you've lost, your circumstances, or what you cannot control. Instead, you look diligently into your own strengths, abilities, and talents for the best possible outcomes.

I spent years unknowingly letting chronic pain be an excuse for not optimizing my life. I kept believing the lie of "One day when I feel better, I can pursue my Thrival Adventure." This lie kept me on the sidelines for 18 years as I simply took whatever job or task was in front of me. I kept on telling myself that once I get past this pain, then I will be fully alive and can follow my Thrival Adventure. But the reality is, my pain will never go away and all I have is today.

Pursue Your Path

The last step you need to take is to pursue your own path. Following the path of others can appear to be a logical and safe choice. The path is clear and well laid out. The problem is the path may not be going in a direction you want to live as a destination. It's very important for you to pursue a path built and defined by you. When you own your journey and find your purpose, you're no longer following the lost ways of others.

Just because someone is traveling down a defined path does not mean they have it all together. The reality is, many people are pretty messed up. They may be pursuing a certain path out of vengeance, past wounds, or pain. To follow them down that path could easily lead to destruction.

Your path should be defined by you, for you. It is a path built out of your purpose and your desire to stop living life in survival mode. Blaze a new trail and live a thriving life. There is no better way to prepare for this modern world and pull yourself out of survival mode.

9

PLANNING YOUR ROUTE

Being Strategic in All of Life

"However beautiful the strategy, you should occasionally look at the results." ~ **Winston Churchill**

Have you ever clicked on a link to a YouTube video because it was something you needed to watch? Say, a video for work, or to learn something new, maybe a recipe for dinner, or how to fix your car? The YouTube video was extremely helpful in giving you specific instructions on how to complete the task before you. But the next thing you know, you have just watched two hours of *People are Awesome* and *Crazy Cat* YouTube videos because you got suckered into clicking on their "Featured Videos" section.

One day, a friend of mine sent me an email of a Stevie Ray Vaughn performance. I love Stevie Ray Vaughn and how he soulfully sings and plays the guitar. I clicked on the link to watch the video. Suddenly, an hour had disappeared, because I had watched videos by Eric Johnson, Jimi Hendrix, and Warren Hayes as well. The music was incredible, and I was very inspired to pick up my guitar and play. But the distraction did not help me accomplish the work I had planned for the day.

With so many distractions and without a specific plan to combat them, we end up following the next shiny object that comes our way. And they come around quite often. With so many choices around us, it becomes difficult to know which decision we should make. If we don't have some type of foundation, some central anchor to our lives, then we will constantly be chasing any shiny object we think will fill the void at that particular time.

This progression through life is having some unexpected consequences because we are constantly shifting our mind from one shiny object to the next. Maggie Jackson, columnist for the Boston Globe and author of the book *Distracted: The Erosion of Attention and the Coming Dark Age*, states, "The way we live is eroding our capacity for deep, sustained, perceptive attention–the building block of intimacy, wisdom, and cultural progress. Moreover, this disintegration may come at great cost to ourselves and to society. The erosion of attention is the key to understanding why we are on the cusp of a time of widespread cultural and social losses."

On top of our inability to focus, we're also taking on more responsibilities typically delegated to others. Thirty years ago, travel agents made our airline and rail reservations, salespeople helped us find what we were looking for in shops, and professional typists or secretaries helped busy people with their correspondence. Now we do most of these tasks ourselves. We're doing the jobs of ten different individuals while still trying to keep up with our lives, our children and parents, friends, careers, hobbies, and favorite TV shows.

The Myth of Multitasking

Although we think we're doing several things at once, generally termed as multitasking, this is a powerful and diabolical illusion. Earl Miller, a neuroscientist at MIT and one of the world experts on divided attention, says that our brains are "not wired to multitask well... When people think they're multitasking, they're actually just switching from one task to another very rapidly. And every time they do, there's a cognitive cost in doing so." The term for what we're really doing is switch-tasking, not multitasking.

We're not keeping a lot of balls in the air like an expert juggler. We are more like the amateur juggler wearing oven mitts, who is trying to throw one ball up at a time and attempting to catch the ball consistently. In our mind we think we're uber-productive, but the reality is, we're barely keeping up. Even though we think we're getting a lot done, ironically, multitasking makes us demonstrably less efficient.

The risk of multitasking or moving from shiny object to shiny object is exacerbated with the younger generation. Developing brains can become more easily habituated than adult brains to constantly switching tasks—and less able to sustain attention.

Young people run the risk of not being able to concentrate on one subject at a time if they keep their frantic pace of multitasking. You need to get over the idea you're superhuman and can juggle everything at one time.

One reason many people cannot achieve work-life balance is that it's impossible to do with their current load. No one can adequately balance the number of balls they're attempting to keep in the air. And when they do drop a ball, there's frustration and anger for not being perfect.

The added stress of living unrealistic lives is unnecessary. This is why you must be strategic in finding your Thrival Adventure in order to accomplish your specific goals.

The Need to Be Strategic

The solution to multitasking is to be strategic in every aspect of your life—looking at your life not just in individual areas, but as a whole.

One of the greatest issues happening when faced with so many options, opinions, technologies, and thoughts is getting sucked into everything coming your way. Or worse, following someone else's purpose, plan, or design for your own life.

Finding your Thrival North gives you direction and allows you to be strategic in every aspect of your life. You need to be strategic in your planning, thoughts, and in your use of technology. If you chase every shiny object which comes your way, then all you will do is chase shiny objects, becoming more and more distracted until you're perpetually living life in survival mode.

When you pursue your Thrival Adventure for a specific task, you begin to know concretely what you're going to chase, when to chase it, and how. This strategy allows you a tremendous amount of freedom and helps you avoid getting sucked into every trap which comes your way.

The point is to stop letting life happen to you. Be strategic about your schedule, technology, health, mind, soul, and relationships. Life can begin to turn dramatically once you get back into the driver's seat.

Schedule

Creating and maintaining a schedule is one of the greatest ways you can become strategic with life. When I graduated college and started my first corporate job, I went out and bought a Franklin Day Planner because I was going to start adulting—and everyone back then had a Franklin Day Planner. At that time in my life, I really didn't have anything to put into the planner. I went to work, and when I came home, I either played basketball or watched TV. I didn't have this barrage of endless activities at my fingertips. Thus, my day planner was pretty empty.

Nowadays, being strategic in your planning is paramount to the Thrival Life. For if you don't plan your day, your day will be planned for you by something or someone else. The concept of "taking the day as it comes" is great when you're on vacation but is detrimental when creating a productive workweek.

Without a schedule, you're opening up your day to anyone else who has a competing priority. You're allowing your life, time, and resources to be dictated by someone or something that doesn't have your purpose or priorities in mind. A schedule is an extremely good strategy to give you the ability to work and do the tasks that are important to you and your purpose.

For more details on how to schedule your day and week, and for your own detailed Thrival Life planner, utilize the resources in www.thethrivalguide.com.

The Power of No

One of the best ways to be strategic with your life and to start living the Thrival Life is to say no—which runs counter to the constant battle with FOMO (Fear of Missing Out) in our culture. You're afraid to say no because you might miss something important, fun, or interesting. The reality is, so what? What if you do miss something? It's not the end of the world. The stress you're putting yourself through to keep up with every-one is in no way worth the anxiety you might experience.

The word "no" is going to be a close ally and tool in your attempt to live the Thrival Life. You need to begin by saying no to the little things. This may be video games, surfing the Internet, mindless shopping, Netflix binging, etc. What are you currently doing in your life that's distracting you from your Thrival Adventure? Are these activities deteriorating your thoughts and adding unnecessary stress?

One of the many reasons you're living in survival mode is your inability to say no. You have to watch the latest TV show, go for a run, or help out at a community event. Your kids have to be involved in every activity known to exist in the community. You need to look good on social media, so you have to be at every party, event, and social gathering presented to you. But then you ignore the people at the party because you're too busy posting selfies of the event on social media.

While all of this may look good on your Facebook page, this lifestyle is impossible to keep up long term. What you don't post on social media are the times you're curled up in the corner of your bedroom crying because you cannot keep up with all of the demands. No one's capable of running this race, which is why you feel like you're barely surviving.

I took a step to take something major, yet simple, out of my life. If you know me, then you know I love coffee. Back in college I had the opportunity to spend a couple of months in Spain. This was where my love for coffee began, for being force-fed this thick aromatic brew was unlike anything I had ever experienced back in the States. This was the catalyst of my coffee experience in which I had indulged in ever since.

So I decided to quit! That's right, I stopped drinking coffee. It was a major step because coffee was such a huge part of my life. But it was also a consuming part of my life, and therefore was becoming a major distraction. I had to have my morning coffee, make sure we had the finest ground coffee beans and a coffee pot that could brew at the perfect temperature, and have the perfect papered filters. This concoction had to be ready to brew first thing in the morning.

If I was traveling, I had to strategically plan when and where I could get my coffee fix, because I had to have its addictive presence in my life. When I finally said "no" to this albatross, I was amazed at how I had chipped away at an unknown stressor in my life. I didn't need coffee first thing in the morning—although for years I couldn't imagine drudging through a morning without my cup. Saying no was extremely freeing. I was no longer enslaved to this little cup of aromatic bliss.

The point is that there are probably a hundred little things like coffee in your life you can say "no" to. You may think it's crazy and not for you. But take the time to go through all the things you do during your day: getting coffee, reading the news, checking social media, having that glass of wine, or television channel surfing. Then think about the time, energy, money, and effort you put in to ensuring you have this activity in your life. What purpose are they serving, and are they assisting you in achieving a Thrival Life?

The Power of YES

Now that you have learned to say no, it's time to say yes. You've probably been saying no to your dreams for too long. You have convinced yourself you're too old, don't have time, don't have the money, or that dreams are for other people.

Begin to look deeply into your life and those things tugging at your heart, calling out from the depths of your soul. What activities or pursuits do you need to begin to say yes to? Be intentional in this activity. Some pursuits might bubble up immediately, but others have been buried within your soul for so long they've become forgotten.

There is life in saying no to distractions and yes to your next Thrival Adventure. Make sure you're using both these words extremely carefully and strategically in order to pursue a life worth living.

If anything in your life exists for the sole purpose of helping you survive, then be strategic and eliminate them from your life so you can Thrive!

IMPACTFUL TRAILBLAZING

Creating Better Habits

"We are what we repeatedly do. Excellence, then, is not an act, but a habit." ~ Aristotle

Brian was in his mid-thirties, happily married with three young children. He enjoyed his job, spending time with his family, and was not fazed by much in his life. However, Brian was troubled with being overweight and needed to lose more than a few pounds. But he had never really exercised before and was not what you would have considered an athlete.

The most physical exertion Brian ever completed was when he was in the garage restoring the latest classic car he had found at a bargain price. But Brian was not content to sit any longer and simply put on the pounds. Having never really exercised before, he didn't know where to start. So Brian figured he would just go for a walk. The first day didn't take Brian very far—he made it to the end of his long driveway and turned around at the mailbox.

The next day he made it a little farther down the street. By the end of the week, he made it to the end of the block and back. Within a couple of months, Brian was walking close to five miles a day. When Brian wanted to push himself further, he started running. This was the funny thing—Brian was pretty good at running and actually enjoyed the activity.

Over the course of the next few years, by simply making this one choice to change an unhealthy habit, Brian dramatically changed the landscape of his entire life. Soon Brian's waistline was what he had in high school; he was running more, and even entering races. Surprisingly, he was winning in his age category. Brian had more energy, was thinking more clearly, and living a far better life than he had ever imagined.

Sometimes, the small decisions we make in the quiet of our mind to change a habit can have the most dramatic impact on our lives.

Understanding Our Habits

Habits are a necessary part of our lives. With the 20,000-plus decisions we make during the day, it's crucial to put many of those decisions on autopilot. This is where habits are formed. The brain, through repetition, puts certain tasks on autopilot in order to not be completely overwhelmed or constantly run at maximum capacity throughout the entire day.

This is why you brush your teeth in the morning without thinking too hard about grabbing your toothbrush and applying toothpaste. You get in your car, turn the key, find your favorite music, and adjust the mirrors all without making a conscious, intentional decision to do so. You have done it a thousand times before, so your brain can take it easy during the more repetitive, mundane tasks in your life.

We create habits to protect ourselves, like locking the doors of our house or car by instinct. Or finding nutritious foods and even working out. We attempt to create a good habit that can sustain or extend our lives. These habits also become useful in our ability to "turn our mind off," which allows us to think about other, more complicated tasks.

Through this process you can also create bad, or negative, habits. Whether you realize it or not, some simple or benign tasks can easily turn into a nasty, destructive habit in your life. The cookie or piece of cake after dinner can put more inches on your waistline. The drink at the end of the day to "relax" can turn into more and more drinks at all times of the day. Even giving your kids treats as a reward can contribute to a weight problem, or have them expect a reward every time they do something good.

We rarely know when a habit has become a bad habit before it's too late. This is generally what happens to us when it comes to the distractions in our lives. We simply listened to the advertisers or manufacturers telling us how wonderful a certain product would be for making our lives easier. We bought into their sleek marketing without ever thinking about how we should insert a new product into our lives properly and effectively.

We end up spending too much time on our phones or games instead of working on our Thrival Adventure. We binge-watch the latest Netflix show instead of making time with family or friends. Or we overbook our calendar with so many activities because we're unable to say no, leaving us exhausted. There's no space in our day to help anyone else, should the occasion arise.

We have inserted these habits in our lives based upon how others think we should live or misconceptions about our own lives. This is why it's absolutely important to take a step back, identify these habits, and then decide whether they need to be removed. Or decide how to more effectively manage these habits in our lives.

There's no magic pill or fairy dust to ignite transformation in your life. Your change will only come about through your daily commitment to a habit guiding you to your goal. This is usually easier said than done. But there are reasons we need to commit to a habit in our lives.

Creates Focus

A healthy habit can create laser focus. If you want to lose weight, then you get up first thing in the morning and commit to an exercise routine. By committing in the morning, you align the rest of your day to fall in line with this one habit. For instance, you tend to eat better and make better decisions throughout the day when you start your morning routine by aligning it with this one goal.

The same can be true with writing, family time, finances, better attitude, or technology. When you commit in the morning, you're creating focus throughout your day, which supports your habit.

This is why I get up early in the morning to write. Not only are there less distractions, but my mind hasn't been inundated by the events, tasks, or pressures of the day yet. I can sit with determined focus and not be distracted by other tasks or competing priorities that usually pop up during the day.

There are too many challenges and distractions in your life to not have focus on the important areas. If you don't protect the space where you want to focus and create good habits, it'll be taken up by other distractions. Create a positive habit and allow it to create focus throughout your day.

Creates Consistency

A healthy habit can also create consistency in your life. If you're committing to exercise, better financial management, or starting a side hustle, then you need to carve out a specific time to work on these projects every day until they become habits. You know that at a certain time of day, you're going to work on building a consistent habit. Consistency lends itself to structure, which is beneficial in building strong habits in your life.

If you're trying to eat healthier, you need to create a plan for what you will eat every day. Without the knowledge or meal preparation, as soon as you get pushed or are lacking time, you'll end up eating whatever is convenient. Which usually isn't the healthiest option. Your focus on your habit will create the consistency to turn your habit into a routine, which in turn will transform your life.

Eliminates Distractions

Focused habits also have the ability to eliminate the distractions in your life. As soon as you commit to a healthier life, more time with the family, or exercising, you'll begin to notice more distractors competing for your time. Your focus allows you to keep your concentration on the goal and push aside those activities that are not contributing to your overall transformation.

This is also another reason why I exercise in the morning. I know the more the day drags on, the less likely I am to exercise. I either get distracted by activities or tasks that arise, or I get too tired or too uncomfortable with my pain to exercise. But in the morning, I can exercise daily without these distractions. The routine allows me to be consistent and eliminate the distractions which keep me from exercising.

Inserting Discipline

In Charles Duhigg's book *The Power of Habit*, he lays out in great detail the reason why we are drawn to habits and how to change them. The basis of his research is this: You have a cue, which causes a routine and results in a reward. In a negative example, you're having a bad day (cue), so you go to the freezer for some ice cream (routine), and feel a momentary sense of calm or peace after eating the ice cream (reward).

This same three-step process can be found in why we exercise, sleep, wake up, or brush our teeth, but also in the reasons why we may overeat, binge-watch Netflix, or bite our fingernails. What needs to happen, according to Duhigg's research, is that you need to find a healthier routine when your cue arises, and which delivers the same type of reward.

In other words, instead of going to the freezer when you have had a bad day, take a walk outside instead. You're not ignoring the cue but replacing it with a healthier or less destructive option. Instead of taking a drink to relax each night, have a conversation with a family member, or insert a time of meditation at the end of the day.

What you're attempting to accomplish here is inserting some discipline and intentionality into your routines, instead of simply letting life happen. If you remember, letting life happen is generally how you came to a place of surviving instead of thriving. Jim Rohn states, "Discipline is the bridge between goals and accomplishment." The discipline is where you'll begin to create a better habit in order to follow your Thrival Adventure.

The two other points to make this successful is to ensure you can identify your cues and have a plan. You identify your cues by asking yourself what is the urge or desire prompting you to drink, go for the ice cream, or binge-watch your favorite show? Are you attempting to numb stress, feel better about yourself, forget the day, or feel something besides the numbness? Your cue will be the marker causing your routine to kick in.

Once this happens, the second part of creating a successful habit is to have a plan. Write down what you're going to do when your cue kicks in. If you don't write it down and prominently display it, you're more likely to fall back into your usual routine and patterns when the cue is triggered.

You need to understand the power of habits in your life and their ability to aid in your own transformation. Wendy Wood, Provost Professor of Psychology and Business at USC, noted, "When we try to change our behavior, we strategize about our motivation and self-control. But what we should be thinking about instead is how to set up new habits. Habits persist even when we're tired and don't have the energy to exert self-control." Without a new habit, we'll always resort back to our old unhealthy ways.

I found an unhealthy habit in my life when I was on the road consulting. Usually traveling to client sites around the country, I would end up sitting in conference rooms or offices for long periods of time in a very uncomfortable office chair. At some point in the afternoon, I would get up and go to the cafeteria or vending machine to get some candy, chips, or anything else that was accessible.

Honestly, I wasn't even really hungry during those times. Working on the road can be challenging enough on your waistline, and I knew I couldn't keep up this routine. But I didn't know why I was going after unhealthy options.

When I spent a few days trying to figure out this routine, I discovered the cue, which wasn't hunger. In the afternoons, I began to notice I was starting to get uncomfortable. With nerve damage in my leg and foot, plus multiple hip surgeries, sitting in an office chair for long periods of time, or anywhere for that matter, became somewhat uncomfortable or painful.

To counteract the discomfort, I would get up to stretch my legs and go to the cafeteria or vending machine because they were usually a good walk from my office. The candy or chips were not giving me the reward. Standing up and getting the kinks out of my legs, and then feeling a little better once I sat down was my true reward.

In order to change this habit, once the cue of discomfort began to materialize in the afternoons, I would walk around the inside of the office, or if it was nice, take a walk outside. The discomfort caused by my leg kept me from concentrating well, disrupting my work. By this simple change, I was able to loosen up the discomfort and clear my head at the same time. And after my walk, I always came back feeling better and energized, while keeping my waistline stable.

Understanding my cue made my reward better. By discovering the true issue, I was putting more effort and intention in stretching and loosening up my leg, which gave me more energy and less discomfort throughout the day.

If you're going to insert a new habit into your life, you need to take the time to discover the cue igniting this habit. Then write out a specific plan in order to be proactive in creating a more thriving life.

Creating New Habits

If you can begin to recognize the cues, then it's time to begin the process of creating new habits in your life. While you may easily recognize the habits of eating better, exercising, drinking less, or quitting smoking, this guide is about creating a thriving life. You need to dig a little deeper to discover habits that are nothing but a distraction—the ones that keep you from a thriving life.

For instance, your time spent on social media. Binge-watching *The Walking Dead*. How much time do you spend watching YouTube videos? And even, the amount of work and effort you put in at your job to accomplish someone else's goals.

While there's nothing inherently wrong with these activities, ask yourself, how are these distracting you from concentrating on your Thrival Adventure? In essence, what is a distraction in your life which has become a bad habit, keeping you from your Thrival Adventure?

What are those tasks, activities, or pursuits which add nothing to your bottom line, but keep you from starting your own business, writing the next great novel, directing the next blockbuster, or starting an after-school program for disadvantaged children?

John Dryden says, "We first make our habits, and then our habits make us." If you don't attempt to change a habit, you'll never see any type of transformation in your life.

Believe it or not, you have the time. You may have to create and insert new, healthier habits in order to accomplish your thriving life, but you have the ability to make this happen. Start by asking yourself the following questions:

- What is a distraction in my life?
- Why is _____ a distraction in my life?
- What is the cue that causes me to be drawn into this activity?
- What is a better habit to insert when this cue arises?

Don't move any further until you have at least answered the first two questions. Over the course of the next few chapters, we'll be looking at different types of distractions and ways to deal with them appropriately. But if you don't take the time now to begin to identify them, you won't later.

11

BECOMING A TRAIL GUIDE

Serving Others to Thrive

"The best way to find yourself is to lose yourself in the service of others." ~ Mahatma Gandhi

One of the least discussed side effects of our modern life is selfishness. As we have moved away from our own tribes and communities, it has become increasingly easy to simply focus on Self. We have slowly moved away from a communal life where tribal thinking and serving were done for the greater good, to serving no one but yourself. This issue is compounded when stress, anxiety, pain, suffering, or trials are placed upon our shoulders. Instead of reaching out for support, we continue to turn inward in an unhealthy pursuit.

The Thrival Life consists of living for something greater than yourself. The more you concentrate on yourself, the more you'll live in survival mode.

One quick way to identify how you're living your life or who you're living your life for is where you are spending your time. A life lived in survival mode is one that is extremely self-focused. You're battening down

Eric Eaton

the hatches in order to ride out the storm. This kind of life usually has no room for anyone else, which creates compounding problems.

The more you are focused on Self, the more your activities, choices, and decisions will be determined by your own selfish desires. You create a surviving life for yourself because you're constantly trying to feed a beast whose only desire is to protect and serve itself.

Being Boundless

To live a Thrival Life, you need to attach yourself to a bigger cause and get wrapped up in a story greater than your own personal story. Your own personal story is small in comparison to the needs of a larger community, and there are opportunities to partner with others in order to create an impact in the lives of people around you.

When you engage others for the purpose of service, you're writing a much bigger story than you could imagine on your own. This is why you need to be boundless in attaching yourself to a cause greater than yourself.

One of the tenets of the Knights Code at camp is to be *boundless*. As children who have lost their fathers in military service, they have experienced tremendous loss that children their age should never have to face. But their loss should never inhibit their ability to grow into a giving, serving adult.

Every year at camp, one day of the week is our service project day. It is a time for all the campers to give back to the camp by building trails, fixing or painting a building, moving dirt, or cleaning up an area. We explain to the campers that even though they have experienced loss, they have been given much, even from this camp. No matter how much or how little they've been given, they should always remember to pay it forward.

At the end of camp, when I ask the kids what their favorite part of the week was, I love to hear a few of them shout out the service project. Our hope is that we're instilling in them, even at a young age, the importance of thinking of others. To understand the value of creating space in your life to always be able to serve and help others.

You can begin to gauge your level on this path by asking yourself, *how do I serve others and do I serve them well?* This might seem strange or you might dismiss this idea, but it's extremely important. All the success in the world is irrelevant if kept to yourself.

Victories are much sweeter when celebrated with others. Failures are easier when not endured alone. We were made to serve, help, and guide others. But in the process of doing life, we often miss these opportunities because we reflect too much on our own problems and circumstances instead of looking beyond ourselves.

Spend time reflecting upon how you served others well this past year. Then be intentional about creating a plan around how you will serve others in this coming year. Many areas of service could be activities you're already doing—coaching your kid's sports team, serving at church, helping at a shelter, assisting a neighbor, or just being there for someone in need.

Your life can be dramatically transformed by your service to others. There are very few ways you can make your life richer and happier than being a light to others in dark times. Don't miss an opportunity to give your special gifts to those around you.

Besides, it turns out serving can have rewards beyond what we could have imagined. The benefits of serving are becoming more and more evident as more people learn to pay it forward in unique ways.

An article in Inc. Magazine pointed out that "if you are serious about starting a lasting business, stop focusing on your own goals and instead focus your attention on serving others, discovering their needs and how to help them. Think about how to create significant value for a core group of people and how you can help them live a better life or accomplish their goals. This approach will naturally align your efforts with the market and put you a step ahead of competition, rather than always being a step behind. Who knows, you may even sleep better at night, knowing you're making a difference somehow."

Even the business world, which mostly exists to make money, has seen the need to offer something greater, work for something more than simply making money. Companies are beginning to offer their employees an opportunity to serve their communities in "Give Back" days. A day when departments within the company can take the time off to serve in a local charity or nonprofit. This article resonates in terms of creating not only a viable business, but a thriving life. The two do not have to be mutually exclusive.

Serving others does not entail you selling everything you own and moving to an impoverished town in India to aid and assist the poor. You can begin by being thoughtful and helping people where they are.

Living a Thrival Life is not living a life focused on Self. On a basic level, we all have this need and want to help others. But many of us cannot help others because our lives are a mess and out of control. We don't have the ability or capacity to help others. This is life in survival mode. Never let life become so tightly wound you have no space in your own life to serve others.

Power of True Connections

You don't have to read much or watch the news to see we're becoming more divided than ever in our nation. Yet, we live in a time when we're more connected than ever. The problem is, even though we're more connected, most of us lack true connections. Without true, honest, and deep connections, we're just surviving.

In survival mode, we try to get as many people as possible in our corner so we can justify our own existence or actions. When we do this, we're not involved in people's lives for the purpose of making deep connections or friendships. Instead, we're there to act as a buffer against critics or unrealistic expectations.

This is why we're becoming more and more divided. We have lost the ability and understanding to make deep connections with others.

When we really look at multitasking, distractions, and selfishness, it's no wonder we're missing the mark when it comes to true connections. When was the last time you went out to lunch with a friend? When you did have lunch, where was your mind? Were you thinking about the messages on your phone, your next meeting, or your own personal problems? What were you missing in your interaction with your friend by being distracted?

We have tremendous resources at our fingertips when it comes to these connections. But in this modern day and age, if we're not intentional about our connections, then they'll never happen.

I'm one of those individuals whose pretty content sitting in his office writing all day. While this is fine for me, I know it's not what is best for me. I need those true connections in my life. I try to be intentional every week to meet someone for coffee or lunch. Especially people I don't know very well. If I don't ever take the first step, then I'll never get to know them on a deeper level.

Some of these connections have proved to be very meaningful. I now count them as close friends and confidants. But it was only through taking the step of creating a connection was I able to create a stronger bond.

Relationships are the Loyalty piece of your Thrival Code—an aspect of our Thrival Adventure that'll keep us aligned to our Thrival North.

If we ever think we're going to solve the problems of racial, political, or religious diversity through screaming and rioting, we're sadly mistaken. We can never create deep and meaningful work in our lives when done in isolation. Change will only occur through breaking down walls and creating deep and meaningful connections, which will drive us toward living a Thrival Life.

Benefits of Selflessness

The benefits of serving others can also be reflected in our health. This should really not come as a surprise when you think about the reason. When you're entirely focused on yourself, all your problems, issues, challenges, faults, and failures are where your thoughts will remain. This line of thinking is not healthy and adds to the stress, anxiety, and worry in life.

When you focus on others, your own issues and challenges seem a little less of a challenge. Every year, before going to our Knights of Heroes camp, I'm usually a bit anxious. Struggling with chronic pain and never knowing how I'm going to feel before I head to camp gives me a little anxiety, especially because it's an outdoor high-adventure camp filled with hiking, rock climbing, mountain biking, river rafting, and a lot of late nights followed by early mornings.

Honestly, by the end of the week, I'm about to pass out. It takes me about a month to recover from camp. But I wouldn't change the experience for the world. You see, it would be easy for me to sit on my couch all day and think about my own problems—the pain I live with, how it has affected my job, my friendships, my family— all of which can seem pretty depressing.

But when I spend time with kids who have suffered a pain I cannot even imagine—young adults who, at a very early age, rise above their pain to accomplish some amazing feats—it truly makes my troubles seem small. I know I'm a better person because of the time I get to spend with these amazing young people. And I cannot put into words how much they have transformed my life for the better.

Dr. Christine Carter, a sociologist and author of *Raising Happiness*, discovered through her research the benefits of serving others. She said, "Did you know that kinder people actually live longer, healthier lives? People who volunteer tend to experience fewer aches and pains. Giving help to others protects overall health twice as much as aspirin protects against heart disease. We feel so good when we give because we get what researchers call a 'helpers high,' or a distinct physical sensation associated with helping. About half of participants in one study report that they feel stronger and more energetic after helping others; many also reported feeling calmer and less depressed, with increased feelings of self-worth."

No matter where you are in life, begin by investing in someone else. The benefits to your health and well-being are undeniable. And there is no better, or easier, way for you to stop the survival life.

Following Trusted Guides

A major part of serving well is to also ensure you're being rejuvenated by others—finding those individuals who can speak into your own soul for growth, restoration, mentoring, and insight. Take the time to carefully discover these individuals; otherwise, you can be taken down the wrong path, or get sucked back into survival mode.

The guides you discover for your own life can come in many forms. The best would be the face-to-face meetings over coffee or lunch where you can engage in deep meaningful conversations. But you can also garner wisdom from books, webinars, conferences, or classes. Each of these methods can provide you with the resources to obtain much needed insight as well as restoration for your own journey.

You may not find one person who helps in all aspects of your life, but several. In my own life, I have certain people I go to for business mentoring, as well as a

Mastermind group of like-minded individuals I meet with to help me with the details of building my business. I have other people for spiritual mentorship in my faith.

While we need to pursue mentorship in all areas of our lives, the problem arises if we become extremely distracted by following others down a similar road. The distractions come when we spend a tremendous amount of time finding mentors or guides to help us.

When searching for these guides, it's important to be careful who to trust and follow. Through my years of finding good mentoring, I have found two traits of people who are worth following. The first is someone who serves others. If a guide doesn't give of themselves to others, they're not worth your time. Their main pursuit probably revolves around money or power. Both are poor motivations for service. Move on to someone else.

The second trait is to find people who offer tangible and attainable solutions. If they're simply waxing nostalgic or talking about themselves the entire time, they're not worth your time. A good guide will the proper experience and desire to offer practical insight to help you on your journey.

Do not go on this journey alone. Take the time to build the necessary relationships around you so you can thrive and not remain self-focused. Then use the energy garnered from these times to invest in others in a meaningful and impactful way.

12

INTENTIONAL WANDERING

Transformation Through Unexpected Adventures

"Not all those who wander are lost."
~ J.R.R. Tolkien

Mike found success early in life, joining the ground stages of a company in the healthcare industry focusing on a niche market. He worked diligently through the years to grow the business into a profitable and sustainable company.

Mike's company grew to the point that a large corporation took notice and offered to purchase the company for much more than they had invested. Mike's company accepted the offer, and Mike joined the larger company to help with the transition.

The transition was only going to last 18 months. But after four years, Mike found himself constantly traveling all over the world, rarely being at home, and working 16-hour days. This new reality was not what Mike wanted out of his career transition.

This was the point Mike decided to walk away from a lucrative job with a prestigious company. Mike had no idea what he wanted to do, but he wanted to use the time to take a break and intentionally figure out his next step. Not one to sit around, Mike began working on his house, started riding motorcycles, was hiking more, spent quality time with his family, learned to ski, and discovered new hobbies.

Mike was also keeping a presence in the business world by helping friends with their business issues, consulting on problems he had addressed for years in various roles. In his early 50's, Mike was not ready to fully retire, but he really had no idea where to take his next step. Mike was learning a lot about himself, his likes and dislikes, through this time of wandering.

Making the move from a survival life to a Thrival Life is not going to happen overnight. The process will happen over time. It is a journey where you need to leave old thoughts, habits, and expectations behind in your pursuit of a thriving life.

This is why it's important to talk about the process. You may take several steps that don't seem to get you in the right place. But you shouldn't discount their value too quickly. Sometimes, in the midst of attempting to live the Thrival Life, you're going to have to enter into some intentional wandering in order to find your path.

Living a life of chronic pain, I didn't know what steps to take or even which direction I should be moving. I kept attempting to live my former life, engaging in work I had always done, and was failing miserably.

I, like Mike, needed to do something new, but I had no clue how to even start the process. Since I didn't want to stay stagnant, I just started moving forward. I began writing a book, built a website, was doing a podcast, writing blogs, speaking in businesses, churches, and organizations. I didn't know what I really wanted to do, but I knew I needed to do something beneficial and worthwhile.

I was in a time of intentional wandering. In an attempt to truly discover my purpose and what a life of constant pain would look like, I was seeing what would stick. All of those activities were not going to be my next career move, but I was discovering what I enjoyed and did not enjoy. What brought me life and what I could do long term. I learned that wandering with intention could take me down pathways I never even knew were available.

What Is Intentional Wandering?

Intentional wandering is specifically choosing a path with the purpose of learning and growing regardless of the outcome. In other words, you're not taking just whatever comes your way. You're attempting tasks or actions which can benefit your life, your purpose, and direction. Then you specifically engage in this journey, not to succeed, but to learn something you would not have endeavored otherwise.

Bob Buford, author of *Halftime*, calls these "low-cost probes" that expose you to new ideas and people doing meaningful work in a specific area. But in the process, you are learning and engaging instead of burning up the entire margin you worked so hard to build up.

You rebuild a car, make your own clothes, work with a nonprofit, landscape your yard, or start a project you've been putting off. You speak to groups about a topic you're passionate about. Serve at the food shelter downtown or intern at a business. By entering into this time period with no idea of the outcome, you're learning more about yourself, your likes, dislikes, and abilities, and all for the purpose of learning how to live a thriving life.

If you have found yourself in a situation where your journey seems unclear, don't be afraid to take the first step toward intentional wandering. The benefits of intentional wandering can be a revelation of a life you've never imagined before.

Reveal Purpose

Part of entering a time of intentional wandering is choosing tasks which pique your interest and can reveal purpose. When you wander with intentionality, you're engaging your journey with your eyes wide open. You're embracing new opportunities and attempting to get the most you can out of life.

Through this process, a hobby, task, or even a Thrival Adventure might reveal itself in ways, or places, you've never thought to look. These revelations come because you've chosen to take a different path and embrace your current circumstances. Look for opportunities in new places.

Provide Focus

Focus is a very specific by-product of Intentional Wandering. When you wander aimlessly, you're attempting to fill some bottomless void. By adding intentionality to your journey, you eliminate those pursuits that may not provide any production. By knowing your Thrival North and finding your Thrival Adventure, you can still make progress and gain clarity in the areas where you need to say "no" and where you need to say "yes."

If you know you don't like sitting all day, then you want to look at more active pursuits. If you don't want to stare at a computer all day, then you want to eliminate jobs or hobbies that can leave you in stagnation. Even when you understand yourself better, you still may not know which path to take. But by saying "no," you understand which paths you need to avoid and focus on where to say "yes." This process adds to your focus while wandering.

Hone skills

Honing your skills can also rise to the top during your Intentional Wandering. When I briefly returned to the business world of consulting, I really didn't understand why. I didn't like the travel, sitting all day was painful, and I didn't find the work very exhilarating. But I was learning some valuable and necessary training.

During this time, my business acumen was heightened. I learned how to engage business leaders and executives on a different level, refine my understanding of business development and process design, and pay attention to detail in writing contracts and entering into negotiations. These tasks were all going to help me when I ventured out to start my own business.

Never underestimate what you can learn in a seemingly undesirable job. When you commit to the process during your wandering, your skills in any given area can vastly improve. This, in turn, can open up different opportunities not seen before.

Introduce You to New People

One of the greatest aspects of Intentional Wandering is being able to meet new people. Through the process of attempting something new, you're inevitably going to meet people outside your normal sphere of influence. You'll have the opportunity to connect, grow, and be influenced by some pretty awesome individuals.

I have met some amazing individuals who have offered me insight I would have never found otherwise. These types of people can have a tremendous impact on you because they're speaking a truth in your life you weren't actively seeking. Their unexpected message will speak to you on a different level and create a tremendous opportunity for you.

When I was beginning the process of leaving my corporate job, I was slowly letting friends and family know my plans. What surprised me the most was the number of people who were excited for my transition. I was about to leave a well-paying job to jump out on my own. For me and my family, this was truly a frightening scenario. Yet I heard nothing but excitement and praise from others.

They knew I wasn't where I should be and saw the potential of the move in ways I wasn't seeing clearly. Their support was paramount in reassuring me and my family the move was another step toward my Thrival North. Never miss looking around when you are intentionally wandering to see who might be walking beside you.

Make the Most of Any Situation

Intentional Wandering can also help create a mindset of making the most of any situation. Remember, when you enter into this time of wandering, you're doing this to learn, regardless of the outcome. This means that even if you fail, you learn. This mindset can be extremely valuable in learning to make the most of any situation.

Time and time again, I have seen people get frustrated or angry because the project or task did not go as planned. This doesn't mean it was bad or the project was derailed. Adjustments needed to be made in order to get the train back on track. But because of certain expectations about how the project should go, these individuals viewed the outcome as a failure.

I see this perception play out when I take people on foreign missions. As Americans we need to do something—build a house, paint a school, or dig a well. This is our sense of accomplishment. But when you get on site in a third-world country, most of what the local people want is your time; they love to hang out.

Many Americans don't know how to respond to this request. Locals will sometimes not show up on time, or are not too particularly concerned if the assigned project gets completed on time. But they love it when you sit down with them and talk, or engage them in one of their activities.

While some people view the fact they didn't get to "do" something as a failure, the opposite is true. You came on the mission trip to serve and that's exactly what you did. Just because it may not look like what you had expected doesn't mean the time was wasted.

The only wasted task is one not reflected upon properly. The outcome of your wandering is not as important as your reflection. If you can learn this trait in the midst of your wandering, it'll be an invaluable resource no matter where your life takes you.

Engaging in Intentional Wandering

To start the process of Intentional Wandering, begin to feed those desires buried deep within your soul. But do so with the understanding that you are testing the waters. You're not going in with the expectation of starting a new career or life; rather, you're trying to see what is feeding your soul and what you can practically do to discover what makes you come alive.

Make a list of Intentional Wandering activities, whether it be teaching others, starting a nonprofit, exercising, public speaking, research and study, working on cars, or baking. No matter what you choose, make sure you identify what you enjoy.

Now figure out how you can incorporate the activity into your schedule. This part will not be easy, but you have to make time for those things you find important. You may have to drop other activities during this time period, as long as they're not important ones.

Now spend some time engaging in your Intentional Wandering and see what happens. This may entail taking some classes to become better trained in your particular field. Or going to conferences or local gatherings to be around more individuals who share the same passion. You may have to walk into a place of business to see how you can help out in order to see what wandering looks like in real life.

Author and business guru Seth Godin, when talking about this process, stated, "Show up in the market and make some sales. Take a role as an intern and answer the customer service hotline for a day. Get as close as you can to the real thing, live it, taste it, and then decide how to build your career or your organization."

Ensure you do not have major expectations around how this time will end. You're essentially enjoying the journey to see where this path takes you. If you're feeding your soul with this activity, it won't be wasted. You'll only be enhancing the life you are currently living.

ELIMINATE DISTRACTIONS

13

STAYING ON THE TRAIL

Eliminating Distractions

"You don't overcome challenges by making them smaller but by making yourself bigger."
~ John C. Maxwell

Kirsten does adventure races all over the world. These races are 450-mile treks where a team runs, hikes, climbs, bikes, and kayaks their way across a country. Kirsten is the navigator for the four-person team and responsible for guiding the team to their destination each day. One of the unusual aspects of the race is that Kirsten only gets the map for the next day's segment 24 hours in advance.

This is why it's highly crucial Kirsten studies the map given to her and compares the plan against her own map and navigation. Kirsten has to know the map, know the terrain, and be able to read the compass in any condition to keep her team on track. Otherwise, her entire team could easily veer off course to unknown destinations. Even the smallest changes in course can cause them to end up far away from the appointed destination by the end of the day.

Kirsten says one of the challenges is to not be distracted by taking the more well-defined path. On some courses, her team would come upon a path that, by logic, appeared to be the path of the race—it looked more traveled, was better suited for the team, and was pointed in the right direction. Kirsten would even see other teams up ahead on the path. Every fiber of their racing mind told them to take the path.

But when Kirsten compared the path with the map and validated it against the compass, she was sure the path was wrong. Regardless of what her mind told her, she must rely on the map and trust the path she had charted from the beginning. The smallest distraction could cost her team valuable time. For Kirsten and her team, the map, compass, and planning are an absolute necessity to rely on throughout their adventure to ensure they're not distracted and keep on the right path during the race.

Amazing Distractions

We truly live in amazing times where you can do almost anything. There has never been an easier time in history to start a business, write a book, make a movie, record a song, or become famous. If you don't know how to do something, it only takes a few seconds to find a YouTube video detailing specific instructions to complete your task.

But in the midst of all this goodness is a problem. We're told to live an abundant life, be successful, and own the world ... yet we're never told or shown how to dislodge the enormous weight on our shoulders before we begin a new adventure.

That weight can be summed up in one word: distractions! The flip side to the ability to be able to do anything you want is you can do anything you want. The amount of information and overwhelming content, which comes from getting anything you want, is mind-numbing at best. Which is why it's so important for you to identify the distractions in your life in order to handle them appropriately.

Identify Distractions

To deal with your distractions, your first step is to identify them. While some distractions are easy to identify, others will be more challenging. There are distractions in your life which have existed for so long you don't even realize anymore how distracting they truly are. You've become completely unaware of the impact they have on your life. Or how much the distraction is keeping you from engaging your Thrival Adventure.

If you want to stop living in survival mode, identify your distraction appropriately. Take the time to carefully and intricately look into the pain points, anxieties, stressors, and overall distractions fluctuating throughout your life.

Much like the stresses we looked at in the first section of this book, the stress and anxiety created through these events all result in major distractions for your life. This is why it's important to understand the different avenues these distractions take within the context of your life.

Change

Change can be fun, but it can also be very distracting—especially if the change is major. A job change, job loss, moving into a new house or a new town, having a child, retirement, becoming an empty nester, divorce, death in the family, or any hundreds of different circumstances are changes that can affect your life.

Building a new house is an example of the tensions that can be created with change. The process can be exciting but create a lot of stress. While I have not done it myself, I have seen the stress it puts on families as they walk through the process of picking out every little detail of their new home. Many of these decisions are not bad, but nevertheless, they are *change* and can cause stress and be a major distraction. Take a step back and see how these distractions are affecting your health, mental state, sleep, or thoughts.

Are there certain changes you're dealing with that are causing a distraction? A failing relationship? Bills piling up? Not exercising or eating right? Identify the cue which is causing the distraction in your life due to your circumstances in order to deal with them appropriately.

Emotions

While your circumstances may be bad enough, your emotional response to the circumstances can be an even greater distraction. Switching from a job you hate to a job you love can entail a dramatic change in lifestyle or income. While the change is good overall, there could be mounting stress around paying the bills or ensuring you have enough work. You begin to battle the mind game of "Do I have what it takes?"

Any emotion generated by divorce, death, or changing relationships can produce enough anxiety to affect sleeping and eating. The snowball effect in your life can become easily overwhelming.

Ask yourself, *how is my emotional state?* Are you stressed about a job, family, or your own well-being? Are deadlines being placed upon you outside of your control? Take an emotional check to verify if your emotional state and responses are being a distraction in your life.

Being able to understand your own emotions and how you react to situations can be a tremendous asset in your pursuit of your Thrival Adventure. Attempt to get a grasp on how you're responding to circumstances in order to ensure you're not getting derailed by unnecessary situations.

Relationships

Relationships can be a major form of stress and cause a multitude of distractions. From family members, friends, acquaintances, to the parents of your kids' sports teams. Relationships have become a fragile piece of ice we all must skate across. But at times we fail to truly comprehend the effect that relationships can have on our emotional and mental state.

When I was a pastor, I had to deal with many relationship issues. I was always surprised by the number of people who would walk away from the church and an established relationship with our family because of some disagreement, misunderstanding, or selfish desires. Each time it would take its toll on me as I would spend days or weeks attempting to figure out what I could have done better. The break in the relationship would cause me to have many sleepless nights.

I was far less productive during those times because the consequences and circumstances surrounding the relationship were a constant thought eating away in the back of my mind. The distractions caused by rela-tionships cannot be underestimated, and it is more exacerbated by social media. While relationships are absolutely necessary, we need to understand the dis-traction relationships can be in our lives.

You also need to be aware if you simply have a dis-tracting relationship. Is there a person in your life who's constantly draining you of all your time and resources? These relationships need to be evaluated in order to maintain balance in your life and your ability to move forward with your own pursuits.

Hobbies

Hobbies, while for the most part are fun, can also become major distractions. As life changes, hobbies can also become more of a stress point than a stress reliever. I love working on cars, tinkering with them, and working with my own hands to fix any issue that may arise with our vehicles. But the more I am in pain, the less strength and energy I have to fix the vehicle. At this point, the hobby becomes a burden, especially when I need to get a car back on the road.

Be aware of the hobbies taking too much of your time, money, or resources. A hobby should always be a way to relieve stress, not something distracting you from a greater work.

Health

Your health can become a major distraction if you're dealing with a temporary or long-term issue. Cancer, chronic pain, broken bones, the flu, or a simple cold can all sideline you temporarily or for the long term. The issue becomes the long-term or even short-term effects. Any disruption in life can become a major stress point because we have overloaded schedules and unrealistic expectations, neither of which can allow for any room for error.

Your health can disrupt your productivity in numerous ways. You can probably remember the flu bug that got you off your exercise or diet routine because you were laid flat on your bed for a few days. If you're not aware of the distraction it may be causing, then frustration, guilt, and stress can all begin to arise. Take care of your health in any way possible in order to alleviate distractions keeping you from being productive.

Minor Inconveniences

Then there are the minor inconveniences of life. The flat tire, leaky faucet, sick pet, traffic jams, snowstorm, losing your cell phone, or a long-running meeting. You have no control over these items and most of them are the results of living in a modern world. Yet they can all distract us in some form.

In chapter 15 "Pack Light", we'll discuss more on how to simplify and eliminate the amount of inconveniences you might have in your life. For now, it's important to understand how some small distractions may not seem like much, but when added up together and laid over other distractions, they can cause some enormous stress in anyone's life.

Categorize Your Distractions

If you're going to begin eliminating any distraction in your life, then it's important to categorize them accordingly so you'll know how to deal with them appropriately.

With each distraction you have identified from the previous list, you can now categorize them into one of three categories.

Outside Distraction

Outside Distractions are generally outside your control. You may be able to influence them in some way, or even quit or change them, but it'll take time and work on your part in order to accomplish this task. These would include your work, relationships, finances, health, and minor inconveniences.

Outside Distractions are the external forces at work in your life distracting you from your Thrival Adventure. Much like the External Problems, an Outside Distraction could be something like your current work situation. You're in a place where you can't change your current work condition, but it's causing rising stress in your life. The level of distraction this situation becomes in your life can vary depending upon how you're responding to this current circumstance.

Inside Distractions

Inside Distractions are the internal distractions taking place inside our head and heart. These are usually the result of how we react to the issues and problems of life. Inside Distractions include your emotions, self-esteem, doubt, confidence, or expectations. These can be major players in how you relate, or deal, with your Outside Distractions.

The Inside Distractions can also be the most distracting of all, as these are always running in the back of our minds no matter what's happening around us. They're also the reason why we resort to alcohol, drugs,

TV, or loud music in order to quiet the noise in our head. Inside Distractions are a major culprit in derailing your Thrival Adventure.

Peripheral Distractions

Peripheral Distractions are those that you have complete control over, but for some reason, you hang onto them tightly. These can include social media, phone notifications, unhealthy relationships, hobbies, or streaming television. Generally, we stick with these habits because "everyone else is doing it." Not our best excuse, but it resonates with us and will keep us content in our pursuit of living in survival mode.

To learn more about identifying and categorizing your distractions, refer to The Thrival Guidebook at the-thrivalguide.com.

Identify Effects of Distractions

Now that you have identified and categorized your distractions, it's important to understand how each distraction can affect you. Is it minimal, can it be reduced or eliminated, or does it have a noticeable impact on your life, career, relationships, or faith? There are really only three different responses you can have with your distractions. You can eliminate them, engage them, or incorporate them.

Ruthlessly Eliminate

For those distractions causing stress and anxiety, and for which you have control over, your first step is to ruthlessly eliminate them. Usually, these are most of the sideways distractions in your life, but they can include the inside and outside distractions as well. Some examples include:

- Unfriending those individuals who are causing hurt or negativity either online or in real life.

- Participate in a Digital Detox for a period of time.

- Remove yourself from the negativity of social media for a short time.

- Learn to live in the moment instead of constantly thinking about what activity or event you are missing.

- Ignore social pressures and expectations. Individuals who impose these ideals may be more lost than you and are applying pressure because they need a comrade in arms in their downward spiral.

Stop letting everyone else dictate your time, schedule, attitude, influence, and reaction. Take control of your own life and don't allow others to decide how you should be living. Be fearless and ruthless in eliminating the distractions causing you stress and anxiety, or keeping you from your Thrival Adventure.

Engage Your Distractions

There are some distractions you'll be unable to eliminate. Whether it's a health issue, a family issue, or even some career distractions, you simply have to learn to engage them in your life. For instance, your health may be a major distraction, which requires you to change your expectations around how you thought your life should be lived.

You cannot do anything to change these distractions, and avoiding them or denying the impact they have on your life won't do you any good either. You need to engage them head on and see how to live differently within the context of your own life.

The best way to engage your distractions is to make a plan to review your life more realistically—look at the sources and note how they're affecting every aspect of your life, career, relationships, and faith. Then use a plan to give yourself some grace as you move forward in your life. The last thing you need to do is add more stress into an already difficult situation by creating more distractions. Give yourself grace to move forward as best as possible.

Incorporate

The last avenue to deal with your distractions is to simply incorporate them into your life. This is the "dancing in the rain" paradigm of life. Whether you have a flat tire, a long meeting, lost your cell phone, or have a leaky faucet, make the most of the situation. These distractions are always going to be a reality and a part of life. And most of them are truly first-world problems we give to ourselves. Can you laugh in the face of these minor issues?

Adding more stress to a possibly stressful situation does nothing to help your distracted state. And it continues to remind you that you're living your life in survival mode. Give yourself grace in this area, stop taking yourself so seriously, and learn to incorporate the minor distractions in life into a more joyous routine.

Intentional Distractions

I wanted to take a brief moment and discuss the Intentional Distractions in our lives. Intentional Distractions are worth discussing because they can provide a much-needed respite to challenging times. Intentional Distractions are those tasks or hobbies that we retain on purpose.

Most people have some type of Intentional Distraction they engage in to decompress from an activity. This distraction may entail reading, working out, a quick smoke, watching sports or your favorite television show. While these activities may be necessary in our lives, we still need to be aware of what they're distracting you from.

Never let an Intentional Distraction keep you from your Thrival Adventure or health. Use them when necessary to decompress or take a break from daily activities, but always be aware of how you're using them and if they're becoming an excuse not to engage in more fruitful pursuits.

Importance of Removing Distractions

Removing the obstacles standing between you and a Thrival Life is one of the most overlooked actions on your journey to transformation. If you're going to have a legitimate Thrival Life, then you need to engage your distractions appropriately. You need to admit the doubts, fears, pains, loathing, poor self-image, or self-esteem issues to yourself.

Review the obstacles in your life. Find out how they have a direct effect not just on your life but on your success, too. If you don't face these head on, then you'll always get stuck unable to move forward, because you'll be trapped by your obstacle.

This is the place where you can choose to be the victor or the victim. You need to identify your distractions and their impact on your life, but more importantly, you must realize what you're being distracted from. When you engage in everyday distractions, you're keeping yourself from your Thrival Adventure. Time spent indulging in a distraction is time away from serving others, making an impact, or making yourself better.

Distractions have become a full-time job in our culture. The more we engage in our distractions, the less time we have for other healthier pursuits. While writing this book, I cannot tell you how distracted I became. I'm not sure if I was attempting to "live the material" but it almost became insane. From kids' activities, social media, the pressure to finish the manuscript, or my own unrealistic expectations around timelines and content—the distractions were everywhere. But I knew I wanted to finish this book.

This is why I packed up my computer and went up to the mountains to a cabin with no Internet. In this beautiful place with limited distractions, I could concentrate on my Thrival Adventure, which is this book—the main goal I was attempting to complete at this point in my life.

Unless you're intentional and purposeful with how you pursue life, distractions will constantly keep you in survival mode. As Vince Lombardi once said, "The man on top of the mountain didn't fall there." This process will take effort and focus on your part. Take the time to identify your distractions and deal with them appropriately.

14

KNOWING WHEN TO BREAK CAMP

Combating Complacency to Take Risks

"Twenty years from now you will be more disappointed by the things you didn't do than by the ones you did. So throw off the bowlines, sail away from the safe harbor, catch the trade winds in your sails. Explore. Dream. Discover." ~ Mark Twain

One of the greatest obstacles to overcome when living in survival mode is constantly convincing yourself the need for your distraction. Another terminology for this practice would be *complacency*—to simply let life happen to you and stop taking the necessary risks to live a full life.

This is where I found myself after my return to the consulting world. While the job was great and the people I worked with were incredible, my heart was not in the work. So I fed my complacency by telling myself "I am making good money," "It is a good job," or "What else could I do?" While all these were convincing arguments at the time, they were also distractions keeping me complacent in my current circumstances, instead of pursuing my own Thrival Adventure.

The definition of complacency is "a feeling of quiet pleasure or security often while unaware of some potential danger." Another way to define complacency can be stated as a *false sense of security.*

Complacency grows out of all the little voices in your head telling you to "play it safe," "don't step out too far beyond the boundary," or "don't rock the boat—your life is fine." These words keep you locked up in a safe bubble, intentionally ignoring an adventure you want to pursue.

Complacency is the enemy of progress. Complacency will keep you tied to your office cubicle when you long to roam free. Complacency tells you not to rock the boat, even when you know something is wrong. Complacency is the quiet whisper convincing you there are no great adventures in life.

Bonnie Marcus, a career coach, talks about the dangers of being complacent in your career. "If you assume that the status quo will remain in place, you are setting yourself up to be blindsided. If you stay in the safety of your complacency without a notion as to what's happening in the company or in your industry, your safety zone can become a danger zone overnight. Changes are occurring all around you that can make your skills and competencies obsolete. Potential mergers and downsizing can be potential landmines unless you are tapped into the politics of the company and listening carefully to the warning signs that change is about to happen."

Marcus is stating that complacency is not wanting to leave a good job to pursue your dream because you think your job is safe. Yet we all know someone, or maybe even yourself, who has lost their job with little or no warning. No job is safe. Still, we convince ourselves our "safe" job, which is a dream crusher, is the responsible place to work.

For years I was trying to live a safe life by working the safe job. I didn't want to rock the boat. Mainly because I live with chronic pain, and one of my issues was I never wanted to put myself in a situation where too much was asked of me, because I never knew how I would feel on any given day. I was petrified of anyone needing to depend on me for any reason. So I pushed my dreams as far down as possible, taking the easy way out. This was the epitome of living life in survival mode. My complacency was a security blanket, which I wore to make excuses for not stepping outside my box.

If you want to achieve more than just the status quo of life, then you're going to have to give complacency the boot. Zack Arenson, the CEO of DECADA Tequila, talked about the trap of complacency. He stated, "Settling into comfort is not the way to achieve this. You might find yourself slowly sinking into a routine, going through the motions, and before you know it, you're neck deep in the quicksand, and it's too late."

Complacency was a killer in my life. I was nearly neck deep in the quicksand because of my fragile living. Even though I had a great excuse not to venture out very far, it was making my life and family miserable because I chose complacency over thriving.

Combating Complacency

Complacency is a life requiring constant distractions. You need to engage in any distraction possible so as not to think about your position in life. This defines many people living their lives in survival mode. They live with a false sense of security thinking that they're avoiding danger by living a "secure" life only to realize there is danger all around them.

In the sport of rock climbing, complacency is literally a killer. Complacency is telling yourself, "I have tied a rope a thousand times, why bother checking now?" Yet, story after story, I hear of rock climbers who were hurt or fell to their death because they became too complacent with their equipment or safety checks. Either by arrogance or repetition, complacency entered the lives of experienced climbers causing unnecessary accidents.

I have found myself about to climb up a rock face being lackadaisical about the pre-climb check, only to look down and see my rope was not tied tightly, my carabiner was not locked, or the person on belay was not prepared. Little steps that could protect me on the rock were overlooked due to my complacency in the moment.

In order to avoid these precarious situations you need to be intentional with your choices and honest with your pursuits. The following steps can help you identify and battle complacency in your own life.

Identify Complacency

At times, identifying complacency can be a challenge. Take relationships for instance. It would be easy for me to say my wife, Erica, and I have a great marriage. We rarely argue, we're on the same page in parenting, and we enjoy spending quality time with each other. But if I don't engage with my wife in conversation, dates, and romantic gestures, then we are more roommates than lovers.

When I choose my Thrival Adventure as to be more intentional with my wife, I will schedule a weekly or monthly date night and be intentional with our conversation. Through this process, I can begin to be aware of specific ways that I've been complacent. Maybe I haven't been engaging in conversations when I should. Or taking those moments to intentionally spend time with her. Once I identify these specific areas, then I have the ability to stop myself and be more intentional and less complacent.

The same is true in your career, side-hustle, or pursuits. Once you know specifically what you want to achieve, it becomes easier to identify ways you've been complacent in those specific areas. Then you can begin the process of combating specific complacency in your life.

Control Your Fear

Another step you're going to have to take is to control your fear. Fear is a natural emotion built for our primitive days of self-protection. But fear in today's world can be extremely destructive, and it's one of the major obstacles to living a Thrival Life. Fear can usually be found at the root of complacency. We fear the unknown, and if we do step out into something different, we're afraid of what might be on the other side.

Pursuing your Thrival Adventure and identifying complacency in your life can be good steps in giving you the confidence to control your fears. Stepping away from a comfortable, well-paying job is frightening—trust me, I have done it more than once. The move may seem illogical and irresponsible to leave a well-paying job to pursue some half-baked dream you have had your entire life.

While the move may seem irresponsible, you want to be responsible in your process. Engage in Intentional Wandering. Do the research, talk to the right people, and put your foot in the pool of this next Thrival Adventure to test the water. You want to be responsible in your actions. Your diligence will help control your fears when moving out of complacency.

I would rather fail at my dreams than succeed in my complacency. Know the fears you have in making the next step and do the work to control your fears, because you're going to have to take some major risks.

Take Risks

A life of survival and complacency is a life of risk avoidance. You'll always play it safe to keep you from stepping too far outside your comfort zone. Risk avoidance only plays into your survival life.

To live a Thrival Life, you're going to have to risk. You'll have to step outside the box and your comfort zone. Will it be fun at times? Probably not. But remember, you're playing the long game and looking for a greater reward in the end.

When my wife and I decided it was time for me to leave the corporate world to become a full-time keynote speaker and author, it was frightening. I had a well-paying job which would secure me a nice retirement. But I was just surviving life—I was complacent because I was comfortable in my position.

There was fear involved, and we knew there would be many risks. This is why I took the time to do my research and got myself comfortable with the move. What would it take for me to thrive in this role? What would I have to commit to long term? Through the process of research and intentional conversations, I became more comfortable until I made the leap.

To say it has been difficult would be an understatement. But I love my life. I enjoy the work I do, the people I meet, and the new ways I get to serve others. The irony is, when you make the first leap and take the risk, the next risks you need to take will become easier. The first step is the most difficult, but the first step can lead to many more leaps to a Thrival Adventure you've never dreamed before.

To make the most out of life, don't be afraid to break camp and set out on a new Thrival Adventure. Take the risk. Whether it be in business, relationships, or life in general. Don't be afraid. Let it be a calculated risk; don't be foolish. But take the risk.

Small Wins

One of the best ways to step out of complacency is to be smart with your small wins. Constant rejection and enough failure can push the most capable individuals into a point of being complacent. The desire not to fail again will cause you to clam up and glide through life.

If you're stepping into a new career, you may want to find an easy client or project to start with before leaving your job. In relationships, it may be engaging the individual over weather, news, or world events. The point of the small win is to build up your confidence enough to take the leap.

Plan out some small wins no matter what you're attempting to accomplish. A few small wins can allow you to take major leaps from living in survival mode to living the Thrival Life.

15

PACK LIGHT

Losing Your Baggage to Simplify Life

"Purity and simplicity are the two wings with which man soars above the earth and all temporary nature." ~ Thomas à Kempis

W e have too much stuff! While some people will deny their plunder of riches, if we're honest with ourselves we could easily dump much of what we own. Generally, we have too many shirts, pants, dresses, shoes, video games, tools … and on and on it goes.

We have so much stuff we have to find other places than our homes and garages to store our stuff! Currently, there are more storage facilities in the United States than McDonald's, as individuals and families are looking for extra space to store those mementos, antiques, photo albums, and excess stuff they've accumulated. In 2015, the storage facility industry was making over 24 billion a year.

According to the Self-Storage Association, "Fifty percent of storage unit renters are storing what won't fit into their homes, and one out of every 11 Americans rents storage." The storage industry is quickly on the rise and doesn't look to be stopping anytime soon. All because we need more places to store our expanding collection of stuff.

We hold tightly to our "stuff" because we think it provides some security in our lives. We think we need to keep up with the Joneses, or could not possibly live without another item we have to store somewhere other than our house. This adage is completely false. The more we buy, the more we want to buy. Purchasing more stuff will never quench any need or desire we might have in our lives. We just accumulate more stuff.

On the other hand, there is research showing how simplifying your life and getting rid of the clutter can decrease stress, provide focus, and increase clarity. This simplification also leads to satisfaction and increased productivity. Now doesn't that sound like a better way to live rather than having to get another storage unit because we can't stop our spending sprees?

The Myth of Accumulation

Now, don't get me wrong—I'll admit I like stuff. I was the guy who always wanted to have the latest gadget on the day the new gadget came out. I thought I needed a big house, nice cars, and the latest iPhone to keep up with everyone else. The realization was that I had to work outside my Thrival Adventure in order to keep this pace of life.

I also found there was no joy or happiness in objects. Nor did I particularly like all the "stuff" I was purchasing. In some cases, the items I bought were only making life more complicated.

I bought into the lie that I must amass as much as possible in order to be happy. This could not be further from the truth. The irony is the happiest people I have ever met are the ones who have the least.

Several years ago, my family and I spent a month at an orphanage in Arequipa, Peru. The children who lived there had been left on buses, in front of police stations, and on the doorstep of the orphanage. They had been left by parents who no longer wanted them or could not care for their well-being. For the most part, they only had three sets of clothes, lived in the same room with five or six other children, and were up at 5 a.m. every morning cleaning their dorm rooms and preparing the meals for the day.

Yet they always had a smile on their faces. They had the most infectious laughs and were constantly bringing a smile to my face. I had never seen anything like this contagious joy before. Truly the poorest people I have ever been around, who didn't even have a family. But they could still smile and enjoy life like nothing I had seen in the United States or Europe. The most amazing aspect was this group had more to complain about than any group of people I had ever been around, yet I never heard one complaint out of any of these kids the entire month we spent with them.

These orphans were not distracted by stuff nor did they feel the need to accumulate more stuff to distract them. Material things can become nothing more than a distraction. This is why it's important to purge your stuff and learn to live more simplistic lives in an attempt to avoid even more distractions keeping you from your Thrival Adventure.

Lose Your Baggage

Have you ever packed too much for a vacation? I mean, you took a ski jacket to the Bahamas and had no reason why? If we really got down to it, we could all probably pack half of what we take on any trip. But "just in case" of an emergency, we will throw in one more shirt because we never know what might happen.

While traveling for business for many years, I was amazed at times to see what some of my colleagues would pack. Especially the younger women new to the consulting arena. When we would head to the airport after a week with the client, I would see them lug their large suitcases out to the taxi. Their suitcases were twice the size of mine, yet the women were half the size of me. I couldn't possibly imagine what they had packed. When curiosity got the better of me, I inquired about their large travel bag. They would then begin to relay the need to have a different pair of shoes, or boots, for each day while meeting with clients. Thus the need for a larger suitcase.

Whether it is shoes, ties, or electronics, you do this with your life over and over again. You don't think you learned to pack heavy on trips by accident, do you? When it comes to clothes, cars, books, kitchen pans, or garage tools, too much is never enough. So we go out and buy something "because it was on sale," even though we have no use for it in our lives. But man, did we get a good deal!

For this reason, you need to look deep into your own desires to comprehend why you feel the need to accumulate stuff. There are many reasons and motivations around this issue, which is why it's important for you to understand what it means for you personally.

One area of accumulation for me was books. I was not a great student growing up and never received good grades in school. This was a wound I carried into adulthood. But I did like to read, so I would buy books, and I began collecting books and proudly displaying them in bookshelves.

I soon realized the only purpose of displaying the books was to show others my perceived level of intellect. Most of the books I owned I would never read again. I was reacting to a wound I received as a young child—that I wasn't smart enough and thus needed to prove my intelligence through the accumulation of books.

Yours could be a similar wound through clothes, a large house, a nice car, or beautiful art hanging on your walls. You're attempting to prove something to yourself or someone else. Dig deep to discover the motivation behind what you purchased in order to understand your consumerism. This is the beginning of the process to losing your baggage.

The overall goal will be to lose your baggage and turn your motivation for stuff into a motivation toward your Thrival Adventure. Remove the distraction of "stuff" to see your Thrival Adventure clearly.

Relationship with Money

One major way to understand how to simplify your life is to understand your relationship with money.

Everyone has some type of relationship with money—whether it be healthy, destructive, passive, or out of control. Where you focus your time and efforts in your life can largely revolve around your relationship with money. There's an old saying, "If you want to know someone's priorities, just look at their checkbook." For you'll always spend money on those items you find important.

Many people are living a life of survival because they're working a job they hate to pay for things they don't even need. But they feel that this is how others live, what is expected of them, or what will bring them happiness.

I'm truly dumbfounded by the fact that our educational institutions from high school through college do not teach some type of mandatory personal finance. Mainly because it doesn't matter what job you work out of high school or college, you're still going to need to manage finances.

Due to the lack of focus around proper financial training, the only other resources to learn how to manage money comes from television, credit card commercials, banks, family, or friends—whose message can be distorted, unreliable, or someone may be telling you to get whatever you want now and just pay for it later. Trust me—you're definitely going to pay for it later.

In order to combat this improper mindset with money, it is important to understand what type of person you are with money. What do you think about money? What do you do with money when you have it in your possession? What are you working toward with your money? These are all great questions to ask in order to understand how you relate to money.

To further understand your relationship with money, it's important to know what type of personality you have with money.

Hoarder

The Hoarder is an individual who keeps their money for unhealthy reasons. Somewhere in their past, they probably had little access to resources, which left them without many of the basic necessities in life. So now they hoard money because they don't ever want to be in a place where they don't have money.

The Hoarder will save money even to the point of not spending money on necessities where money should be spent. Most of these individuals have good jobs but refuse to spend the money they make and tend to live a very modest lifestyle. Hoarders will usually be hesitant to invest what they have accumulated. The stock market is too risky for them to invest in, and risk avoidance is the motivation of their heart driving their modest lifestyle to keep their money safe.

King/Queen

The next personality is the King/Queen who likes to be extravagant and spend money on anything and everything—money that they usually do not have. The King/Queen wants to impress those around them with nice cars, jewelry, clothes, and going-out for fancy meals. The King/Queen usually carries a lot of debt, and they are strapped to their job in order to pay off the debt they incur. They are typically only paying off the minimum amount on their credit card statement each month.

Magician

The Magician has the power to magically make money disappear. The mystery lies in where the Magician spends their money. Mainly because they never have any money, yet don't really have anything to show for what they spend. They live a modest lifestyle, live paycheck to paycheck, and have very few assets to show for their efforts.

Joker

A person with a negative view of money is the Joker personality. These people seem to hate money. They think earning money is bad and they have a negative relationship with their earnings. A Joker is usually conflicted about earning and spending. While they know they need to earn a certain amount to live, they see it as a burden which cannot be avoided.

Sage

The last type of personality is the Sage. The Sage has a good relationship with money. They have found the balance between earning, spending, saving, and giving. The Sage is wise with their earnings, has a good job, spends within their limits, and is never too extravagant with their purchases. The Sage has also taken the time to invest wisely and be a good steward in their giving to churches, organizations, and nonprofits.

Many people will move in and out of these different personalities. You may also find you have traits of various types of personalities at different times. The point is to identify how you relate with money in order to become a Sage. You want to have a good relationship with money in your pursuit of simplicity within the Thrival Life.

Your Sucker Spot

P.T. Barnum is misquoted as stating, "There is a sucker born every minute." This saying was actually mentioned by Barnum's competitor George Hull, as both were trying to pull off an enormous hoax in order to increase profits. Hull, an archeologist and paleontologist, came up with the idea to carve a giant person out of stone. Hull would then bury the giant deep in the ground and have some hired laborers accidentally discover the giant. The "stone giant" was put on display as a must-see discovery, and Hull was pulling in large sums of money from curious individuals wanting to be the first to see the fake giant.

The reality is, we're all suckers in some areas of our lives. We can all think of some item, gimmick, or stunt we paid money for, which turned out to be worthless. Whether it was to be the first in line, have the best, do something unique, fill some unmet need, or a shiny object we had to have off the back of a cereal box, we put cash down on the table in order to see what the ringmaster was hiding behind the curtain.

No one has better use of this type of psychology than the marketing departments of large companies. Companies will spend millions of dollars to create a product. And they have no problem spending millions more in order to ensure the general population not only knows their product exists, but convince consumers to bring the product into their homes.

Large companies have entire departments dedicated to psychoanalyze why people shop, what they buy, when they buy, and why they buy certain products. Their whole goal is to emote some feeling or response from you to ensure you buy their product.

What you have to realize is that everyone is a sucker in some specific place. Everyone has a "sucker spot" where they'll put down money they don't have in order to purchase items they don't need. Just realize how much time, money, and resources people will invest in order to impress people they don't even like. These purchases are usually prompted from our "sucker spot."

You have been programmed to compare yourself, to a certain degree, through these marketing campaigns. And you end up purchasing far more than you want in order to fulfill some unmet desire. This emotion or desire is what drives you to purchase many things you don't need or use.

Ask yourself this: If you were alone on a deserted island with nothing but an Amazon account, what would you really buy? Do you really need a ShamWow, five gallons of OxiClean, or a Snuggie? When you get down to the basics of life, what do you purchase and why? When you layer on the need to be like others or keep up with others, the mentality of need gets overwhelmed by want, which causes some dramatic shifts in what you purchase.

If you're going to move away from a survival life, then it's absolutely important to understand your sucker spot. What advertising messages make you want to purchase something you don't need? What makes you a sucker? Do you purchase items for self-esteem, to make you feel better, make you feel like you belong, or you simply have to have it? No matter the motivation, it's imperative you discover this distraction.

When you long to live the Thrival Life and forsake the message of the world, you'll begin to understand no one—I mean NO ONE—should be able to tell you what you "need" in life. Take the time to unravel your sucker spot and work diligently to block the marketing messages so you're not spending your hard-earned money on a hoax.

Simplify Life

Once you understand your reason for spending, your relationship with money, and your sucker spot, it's time to slim down and learn to live with less. With everything you buy and consume, you're adding a burden to your journey. Your stuff is nothing but a distraction from your Thrival Adventure and serving others. If you want to own your journey, then lighten up.

To begin your journey of lightening your load, here are ten ways to add a little simplicity to your life.

Slow Down

We like to rush everywhere we go. Just slow down and take some deep breaths here and there. Rushing everywhere can make us anxious and add to our stress. Think about items you have bought because you were strapped for time and moving too fast to make a clear decision. Then think about how many times you purchased the wrong item in your hurried state. Stop buying products because your life is moving too fast to purchase with intent.

Declutter

Clean up the common areas of your house to avoid clutter. Studies have shown that clean areas reduce stress and can motivate creativity. Find out how to create unique spaces using less stuff and give away any unnecessary objects taking up space.

Unplug

Believe it or not, you can get by for a few hours, or even a few days, without your phone, computer, or social media. Time spent on these devices usually increases our spending and stress—either through advertisements or comparing ourselves to others by seeing what they have purchased. Neither is healthy and can be easily avoided by unplugging every now and then.

Deep Breathing

Deep breathing is a great exercise to calm your thoughts. If you go on spending sprees to cure anxiousness or stress in your life, then why not try some deep breathing exercises instead of going to the mall. Deep-breathing could be more effective and a lot less costly in the long run.

Meal Plans

Find a weekly meal plan; there are hundreds of them online. Eliminate the stress of grocery lists and attempting to figure out what's for dinner at the last minute. Using a meal plan contributes to a healthier diet and lower grocery bills.

Donation Box

Put a donation box somewhere in your house where you dump your old clothes and articles. By having the donation box visible, you're constantly decluttering and thinking about what you actually need in your house.

Practice Gratitude

Smile more and say thank you. Your attitude, your frame of mind, and your willingness to branch out are all linked to having a better attitude. Plus, if you're content with where you are, then you don't need to buy more stuff to make you happy.

Create a Budget, and Stick to It

Create a strict budget and stick to it. By tracking your spending closely, you'll spend less on the unnecessary items of life and have more to give away.

Limit Commitments

Your schedule is probably already overloaded with activities you don't enjoy, constantly running all over town for hobbies, events, work, kids' activities, or luncheons. Guard your schedule and time diligently. When you learn to simplify your schedule, many other parts of your life will begin to simplify.

Be Present

Being present goes back to unplugging. Whether you're at coffee, at lunch, or dinner with the family, be present in the moment. There's really nothing more important in that moment than the people in front of you. In a culture that thinks it can multitask, we're losing intimate and needed connections because we don't know how to be *present*. Our unhealthy connections result in our consumerism to compete with those around us, instead of being present and content.

Purge & Persist

Once you begin the step toward simplicity, you'll need to learn to stay on track. The idea is to purge what you don't need. I mean really don't *need*. Then persist in keeping a simplistic lifestyle in what you do own and purchase.

Like with the Declutter and Donation Box mentioned before, begin the process of purging unneeded stuff.

Then put some specific processes in place in order to persist on the track and refrain from accumulating stuff again.

I recently took an afternoon to declutter my office, which is the only space in our house I can call my own. So I try to keep the area neat and clutter free. When I decided to take it to the next level, I was easily appalled at the amount of junk slowly accumulating in my office. I was mildly shocked to fill two outdoor garbage bags full of trash and junk. Then I filled another five medium U-Haul boxes full of books as I attempted to remove these unnecessary items from my office.

Why did I keep this stuff? I really didn't need it but was holding onto many of those useless items for some silly sentimental reason. I thought somewhere down the road I might need fifteen computer cables, phone cords, and guitar cables—half of which don't work, or were no longer relevant to my current technology. It is silly.

Purge! Throw it out, clear out your space, and free yourself of simple distractions.

Now it's time to persist in *your* journey. Once you purge, the last thing you want to do is fill up those neatly cleaned spaces with more useless junk. This means you must persist and be diligent in ensuring you're maintaining a simplistic life.

The following are six suggestions you can utilize in your own life so you can remain persistent in your journey.

Multi-Use Purchase

When you purchase something, if possible, make sure it has more than one use. You want to maximize your space by finding items that have multiple uses. Can you buy a toaster that is also a small oven to avoid having two different appliances on your kitchen counter?

No Spontaneous Purchases

Never buy anything on spontaneity. Five out of six Americans admit to impulse buying. Plan every purchase, even at the grocery store. There's no better way to fill your house with clutter than to purchase something you never intended on buying when you went shopping. Unless an emergency, put a 24 or 48-hour time frame on an item before you purchase.

Utilize Secondhand Purchases

Always ask yourself and do your research to see if you can purchase an item secondhand. There are so many ways to buy quality items secondhand through shops and the Internet.

Stop Comparing

The happiness of your life is not contingent upon anything someone else you know may own. Stop comparing yourself and purchasing items to be someone you are not.

Question Everything

Why do you need a certain product or item? Why do you feel the need to purchase it now? What are you accomplishing by buying a particular item? Does random purchasing run in your family? Are you trying to fill some void? The deeper you go, the clearer your reasons for purchasing items will become.

Say No

I have said this over and over, your first response should always be no. Give yourself a convincing argument to talk yourself into a purchase. And then say no again. If you get in the habit of saying no, then you'll get in the habit of eliminating the urge to have to buy something.

Experiences

The alternative to purchasing stuff is to spend money on experiences. As Julius Caesar notably stated, "Experience is the teacher of all things." The "newness" of any purchase will always fade after a short time period.

Watch your kids on Christmas Day and see how long they'll play with any toy. If a toy is still being used the day after Christmas, it's definitely a winner.

This need to accumulate is why we have become chronic shoppers, constantly looking toward the next purchase to get our fix. But a trip to the Bahamas or skiing in the Alps will give us memories that'll stay with us for a lifetime.

Researchers from San Francisco State University found that people who spent money on experiences rather than material items were happier and felt the money was better spent. The thrill of purchasing things fades quickly, but the joy and memories of experiences, from epic adventures to the smallest encounters, can last a lifetime.

"One of the enemies of happiness is adaptation," says Dr. Thomas Gilovich, a psychology professor at

Cornell University who has been studying the question of money and happiness for over two decades. "We buy things to make us happy, and we succeed. But only for a while. New things are exciting to us at first, but then we adapt to them."

Gilovich continued, "Our experiences are a bigger part of ourselves than our material goods. You can really like your material stuff. You can even think that part of your identity is connected to those things, but nonetheless they remain separate from you. In contrast, your experiences really are part of you. We are the sum total of our experiences." Purchases can never fill the void of our identity like experiences do.

When our children were still young, we decided to go on a two-week vacation during Christmas instead of exchanging gifts. We drove up and down the California coast, taking all types of side trips and seeing the sites. We went to the San Diego Zoo, the San Diego Wild Animal Park, and Sea World. Took them to LEGOLAND and toured around San Luis Obispo and San Francisco.

The experience of making memories together was far greater than any toy we could have given them. When we were pulling up to LEGOLAND, we made the kids close their eyes before we drove into the parking lot. When we told them to open their eyes, we thought our oldest son Dylan was going to cry he was so excited. Dylan has never even come close to this level of excitement with any gift we have given him. To this day, our kids will still bring up that trip more than any gift they've ever received.

In another experience, we took the kids to the Caymans to celebrate our 20th wedding anniversary. We all love to swim and snorkel, and Dylan had just completed his SCUBA certification. We spent the week snorkeling, diving the coral reefs, and swimming with stingrays. All amazing memories.

One day, we were going to set off from the beach to snorkel a coral reef about 200 yards from shore in about 20 to 30 feet of crystal blue water. We were all swimming in a line, and as a family, we watched the tropical fish, barracudas, and sturgeons go by us. At one point and for no reason, completely unscripted, all three of the kids dove down in unison to the ocean floor. For me, it was one of the greatest experiences to watch my children dive freely together through the ocean. These moments in life are truly priceless and could never be replaced by any material thing ever purchased.

We need to engage in more experiences, especially with other people. Gilovich went on to state that "We consume experiences directly with other people. And after they're gone, they're part of the stories that we tell to one another." The memories we create with others last a lifetime and can never be taken away or replaced.

Steve Jobs, the man who created some of the most purchased and distracting items on earth, said, "Life is about creating and living experiences that are worth sharing." You have a much better story to tell by what you experience, not by what you purchase. Begin to start living your experiences and sharing them with others. Your experiences will be a true testament to living the Thrival Live.

PROTECTING YOUR PERIMETER

Neutralizing Threats to Your Thrival Life

"Protect your enthusiasm from the negativity of others." ~ H. Jackson Brown, Jr.

Kim is the caretaker of our Knights of Heroes camp. He's a former Vietnam Vet who has spent most of his post-military career as a hunting and fishing guide living in the mountains of Colorado. Kim is one of those extremely hard workers who spends most of his days caring for the land, fixing the cabins, and preparing the property for camps or weekend retreats with campers and families.

While maintenance is a large part of his duties on the property, he's also constantly dealing with the wildlife. Whether it be elk, bears, turkeys, or mountain lions, he regularly works to keep them away from the cabins and common areas. This pursuit can become a fairly large challenge at times. The elk can knock down fences or lights. Turkeys run through the cabin areas. And, well, the bears are bears, and I personally don't want to run into one going from the lodge to the cabin.

But there are also cows all around our property. Cows are big, heavy, clumsy, and not that bright. A few cows can do a lot of damage in a very short period of time—not to mention the waste they leave behind in the most inappropriate places. Kim is constantly herding cows off the property and fixing fences along the boundaries to keep them away. Protecting the perimeter of the camp, as a whole, is important in order to prevent the wildlife and cattle from destroying what many people have put a lot of time and energy into creating.

Much like Kim protecting the perimeter of the camp, you must protect the perimeter of what you have created as well. For there will always be forces at work attempting to thwart your desire to live a thriving life. Once you begin taking the steps toward living a thriving life, it is crucial to protect your perimeter and ensure you're not allowing your old ways of living to creep back into your life or for outside forces to move you back into survival mode.

Protecting Your Perimeter

A wise king once said, "Above all else, guard your heart, for everything you do flows from it." This statement is the reason why you need to protect your perimeter. Every doubt, fear, noise, and junk that fills your life goes directly to your well-being and will easily distract you from your Thrival Adventure. The noise will bring you down and convince you that you don't have what it takes. You have to ruthlessly protect yourself by doing your absolute best to guard yourself from the negativity, stress, and anxiety being flung about in this life.

If you're constantly listening to marketers, publishers, friends, social media users, advertisements, and retailers, you'll end up trying to live the life they want you to live. Ultimately, you'll become frustrated with the repetition of keeping your head above water.

This is why you survive. But if you know this is happening in your life, then you're better prepared to do something about your situation. Take some time to step back, look at your life, and see where you have been surviving, so you can take intentional steps to protect your perimeter from the noise of this life.

Turn Off Negativity

One of the most important ways to protect your perimeter is to turn off negativity. Turning off negativity falls under the Attitude tenet of your Thrival Code. With the constant barrage of negative news, social media, and input from your friends, it's difficult not to get sucked into this mire of negative thinking. Add on top of that the outside negative thoughts of your own circumstances, and the burden on your heart can become overwhelming—pushing you further into a negative mindset, which can be difficult to unravel.

You cannot expose yourself to this negativity being poured out by numerous sources for long periods of time and expect to come out unscathed. Take the time to block, hide, unfriend, or do whatever you have to do to turn the negativity off in your life. Whether it is on social media, the news, or in real life, be careful of the negativity. This includes Netflix, TV, or movies that may not be encouraging or positive in nature.

Keeping a positive mindset is crucial in living the Thrival Life and protecting yourself against the negative nature of life. Peter Kinderman, head of the Institute of Psychology, Health and Society, stated, "The way a person thinks about and deals with stressful events is as much an indicator of the level of stress and anxiety they feel." How you think about and view your circumstances can be the difference between seeing a positive or negative outcome.

If you tend to veer toward the negative side of life, there are consequences to this line of thinking. A 2009 study from the journal *Circulation* looked at data from nearly 100,000 women and found that the most cynical participants were more likely to have heart disease than the least cynical folks.

Protecting yourself from a negative mindset through the road bumps of life is an important step toward the Thrival Life and why you need to be diligent in protecting your perimeter.

Be Positive

A positive attitude is a great way to maintain your perimeter. This is the flip-side of negativity and what you aspire to accomplish in moving out of survival mode. Now, this sounds much easier than actually getting it accomplished, but it is that easy. Every morning when you get out of bed, you simply need to choose to be positive. Because, believe it or not, you have a choice.

When you wake up and it is snowy or raining, be grateful for the moisture instead of being upset of the impact the weather will have on your day. After your child spills their milk, use it as a time to work together because life is full of little messes needing your attention. When your job takes you someplace physically or mentally you were not prepared for, use the time to understand why it bothers you. Are there adjustments you can make, either minor or major, to learn from this experience?

Being positive is a state of mind. In order to be positive, you need to know your mind, which is why you need to know yourself. Remember, in any situation it's much easier to go negative than to go positive. But like any habit, the more you respond in a positive manner, the more likely you are to be optimistic regardless of the situation.

On a practical level, while everyone else is posting hate – make it a priority to post love, peace, kindness, or even cat videos if necessary. Smile and be positive in your life. Just because everyone else is being negative does not make it right. Having a positive mindset and simply smiling more can not only change your attitude, it can be a light to others who desperately need something bright in their dark world.

Shut Down Hate

As we diligently protect our perimeter, we'll see another aspect of negativity, which is the overwhelming hate that's on the rise in our culture. Regardless of your politics, it appears the hate meter in America has gone up significantly in the last few years. With some major accelerant thrown on the fire lately, and this is bad!

No matter how you feel about a situation, person, or politics, hate will never bring about change or transformation. Hate will only bring more hate, anger more anger, and bitterness more bitterness. You have to guard yourself from this hate.

When President Trump was sworn in during the inauguration, I had the television on and was watching the event. Shortly after the inauguration, the amount of hatred being spewed surprised me. I was truly caught off guard at the hatred brewing in America as evident by the violent protests in cities around the U.S. and the hateful speech spun on the news and other outlets.

Regardless of what you think about Trump, or any other politicians and individuals, for that matter, amassing that amount of hatred is unhealthy. Why give someone you don't even like that much power over your emotions? Hatred will never bring about positive change and will never move you into a positive direction.

Be very careful with the messages you're receiving from others, the news, or social media. But be even more careful with your own emotions. Never let anyone or anything take you to the point of unabashed hatred.

You'll never accomplish your Thrival Adventure in the midst of a hate-filled heart. This emotion will be nothing but a distraction that can derail you from your Thrival Adventure.

Check Your Attitude

Your attitude is key in not only living the Thrival Life but in protecting your perimeter from sliding backwards into survival mode. Ask yourself, "Are you angry, upset, or bitter?" If so, then ask yourself why. Do some attitude checks every now and then. Try to discover why you're stirring these emotions, and what to do about them.

There are many areas in our lives wherein we have little control. But you do have control over your mind and thoughts. Marcus Aurelius says, "You have power over your mind, not outside events. Realize this, and you will find strength." For my physical condition, I know I have very little control over how I will feel physically on any given day. But I do have complete control in my attitude and in how I respond to my pain as I walk through this journey.

When you look around at the constant complaining in our culture—whether it be across media, television, social networks or casual conversations—you would think we all lived in very dire circumstances. No matter what we have or how good we have it, it never seems enough because we're always looking at what someone else has, and then feel disappointed or frustrated we don't have the same. While there are a few people who struggle with serious issues, the majority of us, if we really take the time to reflect, have very little to complain about.

What if you simply stopped complaining today? If you're going to live a Thrival Life, then you have to learn to be grateful for what you do have. If you're reading this guide, you probably have a computer and access to purchasing books. You most likely have clean water, a bed to sleep in, clothes, a roof over your head, and food to eat every day. If you're going to stop living in survival mode, it's not going to happen through complaining, rules, regulations, or legislation, but through changed hearts and a positive attitude.

Stop Comparing

When it comes to protecting our perimeter, we all need to be cognizant of comparison. Constantly comparing ourselves to others can be a tremendous distraction in our lives, taking us down a rocky path—whether it be career, money, house, car, kids, or clothes. Nothing good will ever come out of the comparison death cycle.

Once you start the process of comparison, you'll begin to exert a tremendous amount of time, energy, and resources trying to impress people you really don't care about. And most likely, they're not too concerned with you either. Think about how much of your time becomes a distraction thinking about others' successes, and the bitterness that can eat away at you because you have not attained the same level of success.

Throughout this guide, we have been talking about owning your journey and living a thriving life. In accomplishing this way of life, you are not living anyone else's life but your own. You're comfortable in your own skin with your own abilities, thus making you grateful, not bitter, for other people's successes.

Comparison is a terrible distraction keeping you in survival mode. Protect this area of your life at all costs in order to truly live a thriving life.

Eliminate Social Expectations

Social expectations are sneaky distractions, and you truly need to be cognizant of their impact and learn how to protect yourself. Trying to keep up with the latest fads or trends is a very time-consuming process. The reality is, you can never keep up, because the point of fads is to keep changing the trends in order to keep people engaged.

Social expectations sneak into our lives from news, social media, magazines, trends, family, friends, and billboards. They're all telling us how to live. And of course, the way to live is to *buy* their certain product. Friends and family may attempt to get you on the latest bandwagon they've found. This pressure comes from many different sources and can truly become overwhelming.

After writing *The Raging Sloth*, my personal story of chronic pain, I was inundated with people selling the latest unicorn horn filled with fairy dust they thought would help me with my pain. While I'm always look-ing for ways to alleviate my pain, I would have spent months researching all the products people were trying to sell me.

Stop letting everyone else tell you how to live your life when it comes to your home, car, family, or clothes. Unsubscribe from those chain emails telling you how to get rich quick or achieve your dreams if you do exactly what they say. Get rid of those magazines that are constantly trying to keep you up on the latest trends. The *GQ*, *Good Housekeeping*, *Vogue*, *Cosmopolitan* and *Men's or Women's Health*—they are marketers in designer clothing, attempting to sell you something you don't need.

Activities

There's a lot of pressure to have fun or live the "active" lifestyle. I'm all about fun, so don't get me wrong here, but the reality is I cannot keep up with everyone else in this department. In my town, I would have to buy a nice mountain bike, snowboard, stand-up paddleboard, ATV, cross-country skis, snow shoes, archery equip-ment, Frisbee golf, rock climbing equipment, etc. The list goes on and on and on. You can end up spending a lot of time and money on these activities, which could be fun. But they may not be helping you reach your goal and your Thrival Adventure.

Find out how you relax, and have fun and stick to your wheelhouse. There are too many activities in our culture to even attempt to be actively involved. Don't compare yourself to others' activities or lifestyle. They may just be looking for an escape. But you're working at something greater and more fulfilling. Take the time to eliminate those activities that are nothing more than a distraction. Then drop the guilt of not fully engaging in the activities like you would prefer.

Use activities as a way to engage others in experiences. Or as a true escape, which helps you dream and think about your Thrival Adventure. Fun is a definite part of the Thrival Life—just don't let your activities become a distraction from something greater.

Being Flexible

An important aspect of protecting your perimeter is to always be flexible. The success of any endeavor you pursue will be related to the flexibility you provide yourself. Many benefits are lauded in the process of promoting a product, self-improvement, or learning to hustle more effectively, but when you don't add flexibility into the equation, your failure in any area of pursuit will manifest itself through frustration.

Flexibility is the key to keep life from becoming a distraction. There'll be many circumstances in life where you'll have little or no control over. They may derail you for a time. Attempting to live the same life, run the same schedule, or pursue your next Thrival Adventure during these times may be frustrating at best. Being flexible in these moments and giving yourself the ability to make adjustments is crucial in maintaining the Thrival Life.

The following are five reasons you need to be flexible in all your pursuits, regardless of your circumstances:

Realistic

Flexibility allows you to take a realistic look at your life. Take an honest look at your limitations and circumstances. Then see how those affect your life, career, and relationships. When you understand how you best function, you become more realistic with your pursuits. Flexibility allows you to not only give yourself the drive to experiment but the grace to fail and keep moving forward.

Longevity

Flexibility allows you to play the long game because rigidity can be a killer. You need to be disciplined in your pursuits and execution of your goals, but not to the point it breaks you apart. If your circumstances or limitations are disruptive to your goals, then take the time to effectively work within those limitations. In doing so, have a long-term mindset.

Instead of looking at your current circumstances, look to where you eventually want to be. The reality is, it may take you longer than anticipated but you're still reaching and attaining your goals. Play the long game, and be flexible in all your pursuits.

Vision

When you're flexible with your circumstances, you're taking a more realistic approach to your life. As you peer into every aspect of your life, career, relationships, and soul, you're casting a brighter light into each of these areas. The end result is having a greater vision in your pursuits, knowing what to avoid, and how to properly navigate your life based upon your circumstances. Your vision will allow you to stay on the path and pursue your goals despite the challenges and roadblocks that come your way.

Calm

If you're in a position where you're not allowing yourself flexibility or giving yourself grace, the end result will always be frustration. You'll increase your stress and anxiety in a fruitless pursuit defined by other people in different circumstances.

Flexibility inserts some much-needed calm in the storms of life. When you have taken a realistic look at your life, limitations, and pursuits, and have learned to be flexible in these circumstances, you can avoid the pitfalls of frustration normally coming your way. Frustration will never contribute anything positive to your pursuits or goals.

Direction

Flexibility has a great side effect of providing direction. When you learn to be flexible in your pursuits, you learn to say "no" to activities and expectations out of alignment with your circumstances. As a result, a clear direction will begin to emerge. This will allow you to say "no" to even more activities, projects, expectations, or pursuits than before as you begin to refine your overall purpose. If you're not in pursuit of your own direction, then your energy is being diverted to someone else's purpose.

Be constantly aware of the need to protect your perimeter. There are too many competing priorities or pursuits that'll take you in the wrong direction. You'll always have cows breaking down the fences and entering the boundaries of your life. Be diligent in protecting what is important in order to protect your heart and not be jaded by others' expectations.

17

NAVIGATING THE TERRAIN

A Technology Reboot

"It has become appallingly obvious that our technology has exceeded our humanity."
~ **Albert Einstein**

W e love technology! And why shouldn't we? There are many facets of technology which have allowed us to work faster, live smarter, and be more educated on practically any subject we can imagine.

Many of these innovations should be applauded. The advances in healthcare have been phenomenal. The ability to organize groups and raise money to assist during a disaster are truly unbelievable. Even the ability to connect with friends we haven't seen in years makes many aspects of our lives enjoyable. My ability to cook due to accessing a large online recipe assortment, which fits my limited cooking skills, has been extremely enjoyable for my wife (I think).

But there is a problem. Too often, we let technology creep into our lives without ever really giving it any thought—we're not armed with a specific plan on how we should prevent technology from taking over our lives.

You rarely realize how far you have fallen down the technology rabbit hole until the moment you choose to look up. When you finally raise your head, you begin to see the reality of how deeply you have fallen in and the overwhelming task of getting back to the top. But that's only if you choose to do so. Many simply do not raise their heads or accept their place in the technology rabbit hole.

We have seen this problem played out in our use of cell phones, the Internet, social media, and the unprecedented connectivity created to make our lives easier.

The Overstayed Welcome

Think of technology as a good friend who shows up at your door and needs to spend a few nights on your couch. You think this will be a great idea, and at first, it is fun. You go see movies, eat at great restaurants, go to events, see concerts, and watch your favorite sports teams. Because of your friend, you truly are experiencing life in a whole new way. Your friend has opened your eyes to experiences you've never thought of or dreamed before.

But now it's a year later and your friend is still on the couch. Although you still like them, they're interfering with every part of your life. They show up at work unannounced, on your dates, wake you up at night, interrupt your meals and exercise routine. They have saturated themselves into every aspect of your daily living.

The main reason this is disruptive is you never had a plan in place to deal with your friend from the beginning. The same issue arises in our use of technology. For most of us, the use of technology was a slow evolution in our lives. It was fun, interesting, and we were told it would save us time. So we dipped our toes in the water. But no matter how basic we started with technology, there was always more.

This is what has happened to our own family with technology. There was no one specific to blame. Nor did we see it coming. Technology, in its various forms, simply showed up at our door and we let it into our house. We did not put any thought into how to effectively and efficiently control this beast roaming through our hallways.

Technology is neither good nor evil. But how we choose to use the technology and allow it to interact in our lives can either be very productive or destructive. When I looked around at our family and realized how consumed we were with technology, I knew we had to make a change. With three teenagers in the house, if I didn't convey a different view of technology and how it can be used, I knew they wouldn't hear this message anywhere else.

The Effects of Technology

The negative, and sometimes destructive, nature of technology being used poorly is on the rise. Yet there's very little being done to turn the tide of the phenomenon. I found numerous articles and studies on the negative effects of technology in our lives, and these statements about our constant consumption of technology resonated loudly.

- Cell phone use among teenagers is reported to induce the same stimulation as drugs or alcohol. But it's an acceptable "addiction." Would you ever pay a monthly subscription for an addictive substance for your child?

- A recent article showed that people experience the same amount of stress when losing their cell phone as with a terrorist attack.

- According to Simon Sinek, author of *Start with Why*, technology is a source of unhappiness for much of the younger generations. "Young people are increasingly used to 'filtering' their lives and presenting only their best 'self' at the expense of reality."

- Too much time online is leading to stress, sleeping disorders, and depression.

- We are becoming more and more distracted by technology as a culture due to the amounts we consume with no indications of a turnaround.

With this knowledge, I began to see this problem played out in our own house. Basically, we were on our phones too much. This unrealized phenomenon became evident when I rented a movie for the family to watch one Friday night. Halfway through the movie, I looked around and saw that instead of watching the movie, everyone was doing some activity on their phones. With these devices constantly in our hands, we have become too accustomed to look at them for anything and everything.

At this point, I started paying more attention to when our teenagers were on their phones. In the car, waiting in lines, sitting around the house, or in their rooms. Unless they were told otherwise, their natural inclination was to be on their phone, regardless of what was happening around them.

We had to make a change and do something to unlock their talons that were firmly gripped upon their electronic devices. We needed to rewire their thinking so when they go for their phone first, they can think of other activities they might do instead. This would eliminate their constant usage or need to be on their phone.

Technology Plan

We decided to implement a technology plan—a specific plan addressing the questions around why you use technology. Why do you need technology? When will you use technology? Is any given piece of technology adding value to your life?

The reality is, we live in a culture surrounded by technology and it is not going away. Most of us use technology every day and it has become a constant fabric in our lives. I rely heavily on technology for writing, communicating, research, and learning. With the onslaught of new technological advances, I could easily drown in my own consumption.

Having a plan can help cut through the clutter and help us see clearly how to use technology and what specific technology will work best in achieving our goals.

When you align your technology plan with your overall Thrival Adventure, there is clarity around how technology might become a distraction. This alignment also allows you to be very specific in how you're going to use technology to enhance your life.

In creating a plan, there are three main goals you want to accomplish.

Control the Technology

We have an unlimited supply of activities and entertainment at our fingertips. While some of these choices are useful, the majority of them are simply distractions. This phenomenon will only get worse the more ingrained we become with technology. We need to learn how to be in control of what we view instead of letting a device control us.

This is one of the major goals you need to achieve with your plan: to understand your individual freedom and not be controlled by anything, especially those items you have complete control over. The plan is an attempt to open your eyes to see how and where technology is controlling your life.

Eliminate Distractions

The second goal is to simply eliminate the distractions in your life. As mentioned before, the majority of what is available to you through the Internet is nothing but a distraction. These distractions are keeping you from engaging in meaningful relationships and your Thrival Adventure. If you can eliminate these distractions you have complete control over, you can begin to replace them with more intentional activities.

Use Imagination and Creativity

We have lost the ability to be bored. I have told our children since they were young that boredom is simply a lack of imagination. With technology, we have given everyone a shortcut to get out of boredom instead of letting individuals seek creative alternatives for themselves.

A study showed that "bored people feel that their actions are meaningless, and so they're motivated to engage in meaningful behavior. This means people are more prone to create something new, serve someone in need, or engage in more altruistic activities when in a state of boredom. All of which will better serve themselves and those around them." But you're not affording yourself this creativity and service by always offering a distraction in the palm of your hand to keep you from boredom.

Be Strategic with Technology

Once you have created a plan, then you want to be strategic in how you carry out your plan. There are many small and simple steps you can achieve in a short period of time with limited impact. You mainly want to be intentional with how you're using technology and replace the space with something productive.

Clear Out Inbox

The first and easiest step you can take is to clear out your email inbox. Begin by labeling folders and moving emails into those folders by category. Go through and delete old emails. If you're like me, you probably have subscriptions to way too many emails, which have cluttered your inbox. Go through and unsubscribe to the mass-distributed emails you receive and delete them. Especially if you're not reading them and they don't add any value to your Thrival Adventure.

No Phones by Beds

This was a big mistake on my part. I kept my phone by my bed using the excuse that I needed the clock and alarm to get me up in the morning. The problem was all the notifications, which would go off during the night, disrupting my sleep.

I also fell into the bad habit of being on my phone last thing at night and checking it first thing in the morning while in bed. It became a very unhealthy pattern in my life. Keep your phone in your kitchen, home office, or living room. By doing this, your sleep, which is extremely important, will not be disrupted.

No Technology Mornings

Another advantage of keeping your phone somewhere else than beside your bed is that it keeps you from checking your mail, texts, or social media feeds first thing in the morning. You need to create a routine that'll gradually get you into the day.

Checking your phone for emails, texts, social media notifications, or the Internet is extremely disruptive and distractive in this process. You are pulled into other people's stresses, problems, or distractions of the day before you have a chance to focus on what really matters most to you.

Mornings are a great time of peace. When you wake up, the cares and problems of the day have not yet descended upon you. Protect this time for your Thrival Adventure and creativity. Establish a morning routine and ensure your phone is not a part of this process.

Turn Off Cellular Service

When your cellular service is activated, you're going to receive notifications and be tempted to use your phone wherever you have cellular coverage. By turning the cellular service off, you're only checking your email, texts, or social media when you're within Wi-Fi coverage. With most smartphones, you have the ability to turn off cellular service on individual apps. This way, you still have your phone readily available for phone calls. Yes, your phone still has the ability to call people.

This will eliminate distractions throughout your day. You're putting the times you engage with technology on your terms. I'll admit this was difficult for me at first. There was a definite hurdle to jump in not being able to access everything no matter my location. But the process will be extremely beneficial in the long run. Again, you're in control of your life, not your phone. The change will occur with the little steps you take in life.

Turn Off Notifications

Have you ever sat with someone for lunch or coffee and their phone is beeping, buzzing, and ringing constantly like a small out-of-tune symphony? When you think about it, there's really no reason for this to happen.

Go into your phone and computer, and turn off notifications on all your apps and services. What you'll have to do is schedule specific times during your day when you respond to email, texts, or social media. Instead of being enslaved to constantly responding on their time schedule, you choose when and what time of the day you reply.

Use the Dr. Pepper method, for those that remember the old campaigns—they suggested drinking their beloved beverage at 10 a.m., 2 p.m., and 4 p.m. Use a similar timing where you're only responding at certain times of the day. Notifications are extremely disruptive to your thinking and concentration. How many times have you been pulled out of doing something worthwhile and feel the need to respond to something because it popped up on your phone?

When I started this process, it was difficult, especially if I was waiting for a specific email. But in the long run, it has had enormous benefits. My phone only goes off with a phone call or text, which are usually from family members. Otherwise, I'm only checking my different apps on my timeframe and not theirs. In times of writing or work, I put my phone in airplane mode and turn the Wi-Fi off on my computer to avoid unnecessary distractions. Eliminate this nuisance in order to enjoy the life that is in front of you, instead of the virtual one in your hand.

Clean Up Your Accounts

You probably have many people on your social media accounts you don't know much about, nor probably really care about what they're doing. Go through your friend or follower list and either unfriend or hide their accounts. This may seem harsh, but remember, you're attempting to eliminate those distractions. If they're not adding value to your life or helping you in your pursuit of your Thrival Adventure, then take them out. You'll be clearing out a path which will allow you to eliminate unnecessary distractions in your life.

No Technology Nights

In order to curb your dependency upon technology, implement a *no-technology* night in your house. Pick one night a week where during a certain time period, say 5 to 9 pm, the phones are put in a box, the TV is off, and no one is surfing the Internet. Cook and eat dinner together, play board games together, or pick a topic for discussion. In our technology-driven culture, we have lost the art of engagement. The best place to reinsert this into our lives is in our homes.

If you're having a party or people over the same night, invite them into your no-technology night. Explain in detail what you are doing. They may huff at first, but experience has shown that they usually become grateful for the focused time and enjoy the evening more. The benefits are driven by a less distracted life and engaging in more intimate conversations.

Use a Cell Phone Box

Go out and get a small box that can hold cell phones. Whenever you have guests over, have them put their phones in the box as soon as they enter the house. There may be some pushback, but it'll be worth the hassle. The end result is a night where guests can truly engage with one another without the distraction of their phones.

This box can also be used for family game nights or any other times where you want to go tech-free. Feel free to decorate it however you like. Have fun with it. The more you see it as something enjoyable, the more others will gladly join.

Phone-Free Conversations

When you're having lunch, dinner, or coffee, get in the habit of leaving your phone in your pocket, purse, or car. Leave it somewhere it will not be a distraction during your time together. Engaging in deep conversation is becoming a lost art form because of our distractions. Never let your phone interfere with a good conversation. Protect those times with intense vigor. Anything you look at on your phone will pale in comparison to what is in front of you.

Shed the "Always On" Myth

Many people carry around their "I'm busy" or "always on" label like a badge of honor. We think it shows how important we are because so many people want our attention. This is absolutely false.

You can shut down for a while and all will be fine. The world will not fall apart if you turn your notifications off or slip out for a hike for a couple of hours. And guess what—it is all right. Otherwise, you'll begin to drown in all the attention. Living a thriving life is far greater than being at everyone else's beck and call.

Be in Control

The overall point of this plan is to put the control back into your life. Use this thought as a temperature check with everything you do. "Are you in control of the device or is it controlling you?" Be constantly aware of how disruptive technology is to your thoughts, your flow, relationships, and your attempts to be productive in your life.

Technology will never work itself out in your life. Without a plan and a specific strategy, the distraction will only get worse. Take the time to eliminate the distraction of technology and stop living in survival mode at the mercy of other people and technology.

Technology Diet

Attempting to begin all these practices at once can be overwhelming. This is why I suggest you begin with a 30-day Technology Diet. This is not a fast where you rip the cords out of your devices and knock all the phones out of your family's hands. This is slowly testing the waters of a limited technology life.

Begin with four or five of the strategies listed in this chapter, and then commit with your family, or friends, to engage in those specific practices over a 30-day time period. By engaging in only a handful of practices, you're getting a taste of what these changes will look like in your life.

I also suggest you give yourself enough of a ramp up before beginning the Technology Diet. When we attempted this practice in our own home, it was helpful to give our children a lengthy time period to process this plan before we began. I knew we had to make a change with our technology because it was becoming too much of a distraction in our lives. But I didn't walk in one day and surprise my children with this idea. I wasn't ripping cell phones and iPads out of their hands, screaming like a crazy man as if we were going back to the dark ages.

I discussed this concept with them over the course of a month. This time period also gave us the ability to buy alarm clocks and find out where we would dock our phones outside the bedrooms. Most importantly, this time gave everyone the comfort level of the journey we were about to embark. When we began the diet, our family had already come to terms with the process and were much more accepting of the idea.

During this time period, engage in open discussions around how it feels. What is frustrating? What is better? Let your family members voice their frustration or dislikes. For kids who are inundated with technology, this is a tremendous lifestyle change.

I would love to say this venture went flawlessly in our own home and we enjoyed life like Swiss Family Robinson. But, alas, that was not the case. There was frustration, bumps in the road, eyes rolling, and there was some huffing and puffing. But overall, it went well. We will do it again and keep some of these practices consistent in our home.

There's no possible way you can comprehend, research, and keep up with the constant evolution of technology around you. But you can create a plan and be intentional about what technology you use and let into your house. Stop letting technology control you; instead, take back the reigns to control your use of technology.

START THRIVING

18

BEING RESOURCEFUL

Using Creativity to Get Unstuck

"Creativity is the way I share my soul with the world." ~ Brene Brown

One evening in college, I took a friend's Jeep to some trails winding all around the lake outside of town. As we crept along, we kept getting farther and deeper into the woods. Slowly crawling along in the dark, I eventually got the vehicle stuck in some thick mud at the bottom of a ravine.

I kept switching gears and engaging the four-wheel drive. But no matter how much I pressed on the gas pedal, I wasn't going anywhere. Simply pressing down on the gas was no longer a viable option to get me "unstuck" and moving back on the trail. I needed a completely different option than what was in front of me.

We were fortunately rescued when another vehicle came down the trail like a superhero ready to save the day. Together we creatively rigged up some ropes to the winch and wrapped them around the surrounding trees. We slowly pulled ourselves free and were eventually able to continue on our four-wheel drive adventure.

Generally, you'll never get unstuck from a problem using methods that created your predicament in the first place. Pressing on the gas only drove me further into the mud but did nothing to get me unstuck. Yet how often do you keep pressing down on the pedal of your life attempting to bulldoze your way through a problem?

We need to be very creative in this modern world, when it comes to solutions, problems, obstacles, and constructing a thriving life. Otherwise, we'll only create a vicious cycle by using the same methods to get unstuck which got us stuck to begin with.

Changing Our Methods

Albert Einstein has been quoted as saying that "the definition of insanity is doing the same thing over and over again and expecting different results." Unless you want to remain in an insane cycle, to get unstuck, you're going to have to be creative. Creativity is what will help you change your M.O. You cannot keep feeding into the cycle of insanity by sticking to the same routine.

This was part of my frustration in attempting to figure out life with broken expectations. I kept doing the same thing over and over again because I didn't know what else to do. But I was expecting my situation, feelings, and circumstances to change. Or worse, I would do something stupid thinking that it would solve the problem. I needed to take a step back and take a different look at my situation, so I would stop pressing down on the gas with no result.

Creative people invent, imagine, problem-solve, and communicate in fresh, new ways. Every business and community requires creative thinkers in the form of scientists, engineers, medical researchers, technology innovators, business entrepreneurs, artists, performers, writers and illustrators, designers, inventors, educators, and parents. Those with the ability to think outside of the box will lead the future and make special things happen.

Numerous research studies demonstrate that creativity is vital from the shop floor to the boardroom and all levels in between in any organization. What is more, our economic fortunes at a societal level will likely rest on creativity. Erik Wahl, in writing for Business Insider, states, "Creative thinkers know that one's talents are best used to make results that might come from unordinary circumstances or out-of-the-box methods."

While trying to get my life unstuck, I was living under an old paradigm—one that no longer worked in my current circumstances. In order to live a fuller life, I was going to have to get extremely creative in how I approached and lived life.

It's important for you to engage in your own creativity—*and yes, you are creative*—to imagine new possibilities. The Thrival Life is a life which swims against the stream of modern thought and ideas. You won't always be able to follow tried-and-true trails to engage in your new Thrival Adventure. But through your own creativity, attached to your Thrival Adventure, you can blaze trails never imagined before.

6 Ways to Be Creative on Your Journey

To accomplish the task of tapping into your creativity and looking at your life from a different angle, there are six different approaches you can take to begin the process of getting your life "unstuck."

Change Environments

Changing environments doesn't mean pick up and move. But on a daily basis, you can switch things around by doing your work in a coffee shop, a park, or a conference room. Change your environment if it seems stale or not conducive to what you want to accomplish.

When I wrote *The Raging Sloth*, I wrote the majority of the book from a recliner. It was a place I had never worked before, but because I was in pain there was no other comfortable spot for me to sit for long periods of time. I needed to get something done, and the usual method of sitting at a desk was painful and distracting.

For this book, I went out to a cabin in the woods to knock out large pieces. With other work responsibilities, three teenagers in the house, and a needy German Shepherd dog, there were too many distractions at home to get me unstuck while writing.

Try Something New

Get creative by doing something you have never done before or are afraid to do. What you're attempting to accomplish here is to build confidence. I see this phenomenon constantly in our summer camp. One activity we always participate in each year is rock climbing. There are many first-year kids who are scared to death of climbing. But we have run hundreds of kids through our program who have been in this same position, so we tell them they have to at least try.

After some weeping and gnashing of teeth, they eventually make it to the top of the rock. This is the place where their chests pop out, their shoulders roll back, and a smile appears from ear to ear. They exhibit a new-found confidence from conquering some fear they were unaware of, and that confidence will transfer over into different areas of their lives. This reality can happen to you if you're willing to attempt something new.

Find a Competing View

If you are stuck on a question in life or a project, then take your question to someone you always disagree with. This may sound strange, but many times, what you're looking for is a different perspective. Who better to provide that perspective than the family member, friend, or co-worker who's always disagreeing with you, or the person who has an opinion about everything? Now, you don't have to always take their advice, but I guarantee you'll get a very different perspective on your specific question or problem.

Take Risks

As we've mentioned before, you need to take risks and not be afraid to fail. Taking a risk is a great way to ignite your creative juices. Either way, you'll learn something. Like with the rock climbing, many of the kids at camp have been averse to risks in general, so they became risk-adverse in all of life and reluctant to try anything new.

When Jason arrived at camp many years ago, he didn't want to try anything. He proudly stated that all he did all day was play video games and had no interest in rock climbing, river rafting, or hiking.

Jason definitely didn't want to mountain bike. Mainly because he had never been on a bike. So a few mentors took Jason out to teach him how to ride a bike. We pushed him to hike, rock climb, and river raft. Jason barely got off the ground rock climbing, but he got in the harness and tried—it was a bigger step than he had ever previously taken.

When Jason returned home, he got his own bike, he started walking, and he played less video games. He began to watch what he ate and took a few more risks in his life he never would have attempted before.

When Jason came back to camp a few years later, he completed a 50-mile backpacking trip across the Colorado Mountains without complaining. In fact, he completed it in stride and assisted younger campers when they needed help, all because Jason was pushed to take a little risk at one point in his life.

Quit Something

Bob Goff, the author of Love Does, quits something every Thursday, just because it's Thursday. We have too much on our plates. Part of the reason you may not be finding clarity is because you're too overwhelmed with the chaos around you. You have so much going on in your life, and there is probably something you too could quit every Thursday.

Whether it be time on social media, your favorite TV show, clothes shopping, complaining, biting your nails, negativity, noise, etc. Think about all the distractions you have during the course of the day and find something to quit. But quit something with the intention of giving yourself a creative space to concentrate on your Thrival Adventure.

Journal

Writing is a funnel that can release more thoughts when you're stuck. Writing is a wonderful tool in opening the creative juices to try something different. I see people accomplish this in varying ways, whether it is straight writing, Sketchnotes outlines, sticky notes, a whiteboard, Kanban board, or jots on paper. How you do it is not as important as creating a consistent habit of journaling.

If you're going to venture out on a new path, it's imperative you exercise creativity. You'll hit all types of obstacles you never planned or saw coming, but don't get stuck in the process. Instead, get creative in your attempt to find a solution to get you unstuck, as you strive to live the Thrival Life.

19

ENJOY THE JOURNEY

A Reflective Adventure

"Learning without reflection is a waste. Reflection without learning is dangerous." ~ Confucius

My hands tightly gripped the steering wheel of a brand-new Dodge Challenger. The engine rumbled every time I pressed down on the accelerator. As I stared down the quarter-mile straightaway waiting for the light to turn green, my heart was rapidly racing.

In one of those bucket list moments of life, I had the opportunity to race down a quarter-mile track at Bandimere Speedway in Denver. It was an experience which certainly did not let me down.

When you're waiting at the starting line, your full concentration is dedicated to the light pole sitting before you. As you watch the lights go from red, yellow, and then green, time appears to slow down. Your entire body is consumed with the anticipation of punching down on the gas pedal.

When the light turned green, I stomped my foot down as fast and hard as possible on the accelerator. I gripped the steering wheel tightly and held on. My attention moved from the green light to completely being focused on the end of the track and crossing the finish line. Hopefully with a time that wouldn't be too embarrassing.

The entire sprint only took 14 seconds as I accelerated up to 114 mph. In a flash, the race was over, and I was slowing down the car to turn around and head back to the starting line.

In the midst of these rapid adventures, we rarely have time to think or concentrate on anything other than the task in front of us. To maintain our pace, it is imperative we focus on the straightaway so we can cross the finish line. The problem is, in the midst of the race, there's very little time to think about anything else.

In our own lives, we tend to go 100 mph without a thought about where we are going, why we are going in a certain direction, and what purpose it serves. We rarely take the time to slow down and reflect upon the good and bad in life in the midst of certain circumstances. When we move through life at a blistering pace, we're generally missing out on the better things life has to offer.

In my own life, I want to be as productive as possible. But I rarely incite change in the midst of the cacophony of life. On the other hand, when I attempt to steal away for quiet and peace, great things happen. When I can spend a few days in the mountains in reflection, problems become clearer, pathways begin to form, and issues I thought were insurmountable do not seem as large.

The epitome of survival mode is attempting to make decisions and choices in the midst of the chaos of life. To try to work on a dozen other problems while going 100 mph down the track. You probably don't make the best decisions during these times. Don't be afraid to take a step back and engage life from the perspective of quiet reflection. You might find creative solutions you never thought possible.

Meditation

Meditation, or deep breathing, is a great way to begin the process of engaging in a reflective life. Many recent studies show that the benefits of meditation are through the roof. "Meditation can give you a sense of calm, peace, and balance that benefits both your emotional well-being and your overall health. When you meditate, you clear away the information overload that builds up every day and contributes to your stress." Meditation, which is simply clearing your thoughts from the frenetic antics of life, can put you on a much-needed pathway of peace and calm.

Writer Kevin Loria says, "Multiple studies have shown that meditation can help reduce levels of depression and anxiety, along with helping people tolerate pain better. The researchers conclude that mindfulness meditation in particular might help people deal with psychological stress."

Many CEOs, executives, and high-performing indi-viduals have incorporated mediation into their daily routine. They realize the overwhelming stress their jobs can create and know that without some outlet of calming peace, their careers would be short-lived. Meditation is a tool to not only keep them in the game, but to be effective in the process.

"One of the most interesting studies in the last few years carried out at Yale University found that mindfulness meditation decreases activity in the default mode network (DMN), the brain network responsible for mind-wandering and self-referential thoughts – a.k.a., 'monkey mind.' The DMN is 'on' or active when we're not thinking about anything in particular, when our minds are just wandering from thought to thought."

Researches are realizing that meditation provides immense focus. Instead of letting your mind wander to a thousand different places, which can cause worry, stress, or anxiety, rely on concentrated meditation to eliminate the wandering mind and focus more clearly on the important tasks at hand.

"Since mind-wandering is typically associated with being less happy, ruminating, and worrying about the past and future, it's the goal for many people to dial it down. Several studies have shown that meditation, through its quieting effect on the DMN, appears to do just this. And even when the mind does start to wander, because of the new connections that form, meditators are better at snapping back out of it."

Meditation may take different forms for you, like deep-breathing, taking a quiet walk, or repetitive reading of encouraging thoughts. The point is to calm yourself in order to find peace which cannot be attained while moving at a 100-mph pace. To help with creativity, simplicity, and all the other areas, you need to learn to slow down, take it easy, and engage in meditation and reflection upon your life. The alternative is constantly living life in survival mode and jumping aimlessly from one activity to the next.

The Lost Art of Being Bored

Boredom is really a lack of creativity. If you're creative, then you'll never be bored. As mentioned before, boredom is where your mind begins to work, process, and figure a way out of your boredom. Boredom is truly one of the greatest gifts you could ever give yourself.

By constantly keeping your children busy, you're denying them this gift. In turn, these children will turn into adults who have never learned how to process still times effectively—to create their way out of boredom and discover new truths about life and themselves.

Children also don't learn how to simply sit still. You'll rarely learn the greater things about yourself in the hurried frenetic pace of life. Consequently, it is in those still moments your greatest areas of growth can be illuminated.

Wijnand van Tilburg, from the University of Limerick, co-author of the paper *"Bored George Helps Others,"* reported that "Boredom makes people long for different and purposeful activities, and as a result they turn towards more challenging and meaningful activities, turning towards what they perceive to be really meaningful in life."

Turns out, boredom is actually good for you. Early in my career while doing computer programming, I would often get in the car and drive around with the radio off to seek clarity on solving a current problem. These days, I often take a walk or go for a hike in the midst of writing or preparing for a talk. The time alone and being bored allow my thoughts to center and gain clarity on effectively completing the task.

Don't over-plan every day of your life to the point you have no place or time to be bored. Mark out large portions of your calendar and do nothing. Let your creative juices flow and see where your journey takes you. Boredom could be one of the greatest weapons you choose to fight against living life in survival mode.

Power of Reflection

Reflection is another powerful tool in your pursuit of the Thrival Life. During these times of reflection, creative solutions to problems can begin to form—solutions which would have never been found without slowing down the pace of life, if even for a moment. Build consistent space in your life to reflect on your time, life, pursuits, and what you have achieved. Your time of reflection will provide direction and balance.

Use your time of reflection with the intention to reach a specific purpose in pursuing a Thrival Life.

Self-Check

The most important area you can reflect on is your own health. Complete a self-check to see how you are doing mentally, physically, emotionally, and spiritually. Are you keeping yourself in balance? Is some part of your life out of whack and in need of realigning? A self-check of your health is difficult to accomplish on a crowded subway ride home after a long day at the office but much more attainable in the quiet places of life.

John Locke said, "Education begins the gentleman, but reading, good company, and reflection must finish him." Your knowledge and abilities are only a piece of the puzzle—one that is fully rounded out through times of self-reflection.

Take the time to reflect on how you have been burning your candle. Are you stressed without any idea how to move past your current situation? Have you given up on trying to eat right and exercise? Does the idea of spending time with extended family for a week send you over the edge? Have there been major events in your life over the past year that you haven't dealt with properly, like the loss of a loved one, divorce, or other major life changes?

These situations can have a dramatic effect on your life and health, and need to be dealt with appropriately. Think about those major circumstances weighing you down, and then seek guidance on how to walk through the healing process properly. If you don't take the time to deal with these situations, they'll eventually come back to haunt you, usually at the worst possible time. Get a jump on your own transformation by dealing with your own care head on.

Successes

Next, you also need to reflect upon your successes. Where did you do exceptionally well this past year? Take the time to write these events down and give yourself a pat on the back. Whether it was starting a new company, a great vacation with the family, time with your spouse or kids, a promotion, or completion of a major project, remember to celebrate and feel proud of what you did well over this past year.

There are two reasons to reflect upon your success, and the first is to remember what you did well. Despite any negatives or failures you might have had over the past year, you've also accomplished some great feats, which should be remembered.

The second reason is you want to be able to replicate these feats as much as possible over the coming year. You may not be able to do an exact copy, but you have learned something important during the process of achieving something great.

Failures

Now, you want to take some time to reflect upon your failures—those times where you missed the mark. The purpose of this exercise is not to beat yourself up over the areas where you have failed but to gain an understanding on why you failed and what you can do to correct the situation moving forward.

There may be failures that were out of your control, so don't reflect long on those. Look at the ones where you could have done something differently. Did you need accountability, a better plan, more forethought, someone to give you feedback around an idea, or take a more strategic position? The main point is to look for opportunities for growth. You don't want to make the same mistakes moving forward.

You can easily dismiss this chapter, especially if you're a Type-A extrovert. But everyone can use a little time of meditation and reflection in their lives. Do not dismiss this work; instead, discover different ways meditation and reflection can be incorporated into your life.

20

SETTING YOUR PACE

Finding Rhythm in Life

"Procrastination is one of the most common and deadliest diseases and its toll on happiness and success is heavy." ~ Wayne Gretzky

There's something unexplainable about the feeling of riding your mountain bike down a dirt trail surrounded by trees with no one around as a distraction. While I love to mountain bike, I really don't enjoy riding with other people. I'm always the slowest one in the group—especially in a town full of world class mountain bikers who have world championships, Olympic medals, and professional sponsorships to their names.

Occasionally, I'll get asked to go for a ride, but I generally say no. Their response is usually "No, it'll be fine. I'm not planning on going that fast." But there's still a wide gap between their slow and my fast.

If I do ride with someone, I push myself as hard as possible and still I'm way behind the pack and becoming increasingly exhausted. The ride itself is not very enjoyable because I'm riding way outside my own rhythm. But when I ride by myself, or with those few individuals who are at my speed, the ride becomes an extremely enjoyable experience due to the fact I'm riding at my own comfortable pace.

Recognizing the pace with which your life is moving forward is extremely important. Too fast, and you could fall on your face or miss some important events. Too slow, and you could miss events altogether or you get too far behind. This is your life, and it's important to move at your own pace, to find your own unique rhythm. You cannot move at someone else's pace and expect the same results.

Face Fear

In setting your own pace, one of the huge hurdles you have to jump over is facing your fears. In chapter 14, "Protecting Your Perimeter," we talked about controlling your fears in order to build your confidence. In this chapter, however, you need to face the fears that are creating excuses and distractions in your life. Everyone has some type of fear that comes from past experiences. You could have a fear of failure, being discovered as a fraud, opening yourself up to others, or not being liked. These fears are reasons why you've chosen to live a complacent life.

One of the problems with living in survival mode is you have to work really hard. Because of your fear, you have chosen to live life in a safe cocoon—but it's exhausting trying to keep up the pace with everyone else, and it's draining to live a life devoid of passion or personal pursuits.

To set your own pace in life, you need to face your fears head on, or you'll live the rest of your life attempting to keep your head above water.

This includes our good friend FOMO. Honestly, until recently I had never even heard of FOMO. I assumed it was one of those technology conferences out in San Francisco.

FOMO is the acronym for Fear of Missing Out, and is defined as a "form of social anxiety, whereby one is compulsively concerned that one might miss an opportunity for social interaction, a novel experience, profitable investment or other satisfying event." Several recent articles in Forbes and the Washington Post show that FOMO is causing some very unhealthy behavior in our lives.

In living a life of FOMO, you're constantly chasing shiny objects and other people's dreams. By definition, you're unable to find your own rhythm because you're constantly waiting for the next great thing to come along. FOMO is the epitome of survival mode and causes an extremely unbalanced life.

FOMO All Around

Because of FOMO, we push ourselves to the point of exhaustion, or we over-stretch ourselves because we're so afraid we might miss an event, a party, or an experience. This cycle constantly keeps us out of rhythm in pursuing our adventure.

I was fortunate enough to sit in on a talk with a firm that specializes in studying millennials and their subsequent FOMO. They discussed how Wal-Mart and other major corporations have to rethink their performance management strategies because millennials will refuse a promotion for fear of what they might miss, or have to give up, due to the extra workload.

But the more I looked into FOMO, the more I see that the issue is not just a younger generation problem. Many parents are pushing their children too hard and too fast in school, sports, and other extracurricular activities because they fear their child might be missing out on an experience. They overload their child's schedule with AP classes because they want their child to get into an Ivy League university, or they put them into sports activities that consume all their afternoons and weekends—all the while trying to claim that their child is above average, which seems strange since neither of the parents are above average.

This may sound harsh, but this is what happens when we have the fear of missing out, or fear of our children missing out. We'll go through extraordinary lengths to make sure we do not ever let that happen, to the detriment of living a thriving life.

This fear is born out of our inability to truly identify our true self. We're constantly searching for some event or activity we think will fill the void left in our soul. But when you're living in fear, you're never satisfied. You will always be searching for the next event or activity because the current one will no longer fill the need it once claimed. The distraction this pursuit creates will constantly keep you out of rhythm and focused on items which do not matter.

Remember you have a Thrival Adventure; you are simplifying life and eliminating distractions. You are no longer concerned with other people's successes, but investing fully into your own life. Following closely those individuals who have yet to clearly define their own path is a dangerous and perilous journey at best.

Avoid Procrastination

Another area worth exploring when setting your own pace is to avoid procrastination. Procrastination has killed the greatest intentions and worthwhile pursuits.

I really can't think of a time in my life where procrastinating really paid off. But, there's a long list of times where procrastinating really made my life difficult.

In college, I was always putting off my papers until the night before they were due. I was either up all night or until the late hours cranking out a paper I had been given weeks to complete.

During my senior year, on the last paper I was to turn in before graduation, I dug into the task early—so early that I was finished several days before it was due. At first, I almost panicked. *Did I get the assignment right? Did I do the right research?* And I even thought, *did I write the correct paper?*

After the initial swelling of panic and emotional upheaval, a strange sense of calm came over me. I then began to think why I'd never completed a paper this early before. Why did I always wait until the last minute to complete my papers? The procrastination caused stress, worry, and many unnecessary sleepless nights.

Dr. Joseph Ferrari, Ph.D., associate professor of psychology at De Paul University in Chicago, spent many years studying procrastination. He identified three main reasons why people procrastinate. The first relate to those individuals who love the rush of putting off tasks or projects until the last minute. These people get some type of high from working under pressure, so they intentionally wait until the last minute to get the rush of completing a complicated assignment right under the due date.

The second group is those who fear success and failure because they're greatly concerned with what others think of them. By procrastinating, they would rather have others view them as lazy instead of incapable.

The last group simply cannot make a decision. By making no decision, they have absolved themselves of the responsibility of the outcome of any decision. You can usually find these people in a crowd by asking the simple question of "Where do you want to go for dinner?" Crying out in unison, you will hear the famed response of "I don't care."

We can all admit we have procrastinated on some activity in our lives. But the longer we put off our pursuit of the Thrival Life, the longer we will live in survival mode—which is no place to live life.

You need to be more action-oriented. As author Brian Tracy states, "You need to overcome procrastination, push aside your fears and launch 100% toward the achievement of your most important goals. The combination of goal orientation, result orientation and action orientation, in themselves will virtually assure great success." When you have a defined Thrival Adventure and a solid strategy, it becomes easier to avoid procrastination because you're working toward a greater purpose.

Find Your Rhythm

The last aspect of setting your pace is to find your rhythm. Finding your rhythm can best be accomplished by asking the following:

- "When do you work best?"

- "How do you work best?"

- "Where do you work best?"

These three questions can help you identify the best way to accomplish your Thrival Adventure and pursuits. How does your goal fit in with the rest of your life, and how are you going to manage it properly? This principle is extremely important and a key element of living the Thrival Life.

How can you create intentional interruptions, which will help you readjust, for the sole purpose of being able to get back to your tasks or goals with the same vigor and intensity? This will take some experimentation, but once you can find a rhythm, you'll enter a flow and complete your goals in a timely manner.

You have to understand what time of day works best for you or when you do your best work because it may also be the time that offers the least amount of distractions. Take a moment to discover how you work best—do you do well under pressure? Do you need your space or some place in between?

Also, know where you work best—is it in a quiet space like a library, or do you need to be in a coffee shop around other people? Or perhaps off in a cabin away from everyone.

I know it's extremely difficult to attempt to cultivate a Thrival Life when you have careers, children, family, TV, social media, sicknesses, and any of a number of other distractions keeping you from your goal. The point here is not to let this be an exercise in frustration, but keep at it as much as possible until you can find a rhythm which works for you. Your rhythm may be crazy and completely unsustainable for anyone else, but if it works for you, then awesome! Keep at it.

Stop living in survival mode because you're running someone else's race. Set your own pace in order to create your Thrival Adventure, and on the timing which best suits your end result.

21

EMBRACING YOUR ADVENTURE

Living an Authentic Life

**"The privilege of a lifetime is to become
who you truly are."** ~ Carl Jung

The greatest tragedy in our lives is to live someone else's adventure—to not work diligently toward our own goals using the talents bestowed upon us to maximum potential. In the barrage of messages we receive on a daily basis, it's easy to get lost in the attempt to understand who we are. The irony is, no one likes a phony ... and yet, we are confused as to how we can live authentically.

We have perfected the inauthentic life in our modern culture. With social media, anyone can display a perfect version of themselves. We, as the viewers, believe what they are posting and take it as truth, like some reality TV show. But their life could be messy behind the scenes, and they could have no clue as to how to climb back out of the hole in which they have fallen.

Having counseled people for many years across many different age, ethnic, and social groups, one thing

I have learned is you really never know what goes on behind closed doors. Some of the most damaged, hurtful people have learned how to function effectively in society. Their "mask" is their ability to portray a healthy image of themselves to others.

This is where recognition becomes extremely important—to recognize who you really are, how you're attempting to live like someone else, and how you can live a more authentic life. The more you try to live someone else's life, the more stress and anxiety will compound. The stress results from the recognition that deep down in your soul, you know you're hiding something, and you're afraid others will not like you if you revealed your true self.

Discovering Authenticity

You need to discover authenticity in your life. When everything is peeled away, who are you deep down inside? While it may be a scary question to ask, you need to get to the answer.

This is also not an easy process. I have met with numerous people who wanted to change, but when met with the reality of transformation, they ran away as fast as possible.

In discovering your own authenticity, if you like what you see, then begin to live from that place. If you don't like what you see when everything is pulled away, then it's time to make a change. Either way, you're making progress to a more thriving life and abandoning your survival syndrome.

Sometimes people attempt to emulate others whom they think are living the perfect life. The irony is the person you want to emulate probably has more problems than you can even imagine. They are projecting some awesome lifestyle or persona to cover up much of the hurt inside them that they don't know how to deal with.

Think about all the recent stories about inappropriate sexual behavior. Once-respected people like Bill Cosby; Jared Fogle, the Subway spokesperson; and more recently, Hollywood producer Harvey Weinstein. There are also a number of other celebrities whose lives seem to be unraveling before our eyes. They were all hiding in plain sight, projecting a functioning lifestyle, but each had a dark secret they were hiding from the general public.

When we choose to wear our masks over living an authentic life, hurt will always follow close behind. This is a topic which could be encased in an entire series of books. Creating an authentic life is a monumental effort. But if you truly want to change and transform, then begin the process of finding a safe place where you can begin to find the authentic you.

Living Authentically

Once you have discovered who you are, then you need to live authentically. Trying to be anyone else is absolutely exhausting and a complete waste of energy. There's no point to it. You're expending way too much energy on a frivolous pursuit.

But if you truly want to thrive, then you can live authentically with the best traits which have been given to you. You might be a little awkward, weird, nerdy, or laugh too much. But that is great. Let the world see the true you. I guarantee they will love the real you.

Living authentically is living out of your true self. Stop the facade of living a life you don't enjoy, don't even understand, and live as the person you were born and created to be.

Social media, and the media in general, has so skewed this concept that it has become truly difficult to understand. You think you have to portray some act instead of being honest about how you feel or what you want to do. Inauthenticity deteriorates relationships and our understanding of each other.

The irony is that most people are truly drawn to an authentic individual—a person who has taken the time to discover themselves and are not too concerned with what others think. The attraction is to create this authenticity in our own lives.

While we may not be able to change the world, we can change our little world. When you choose to stop trying to be someone else, you're living an authentic life. Any other way of living is simply living in survival mode.

Drowning Out the Noise

One of the greatest challenges in living an authentic life is drowning out the noise. Unless you live on an isolated island with no TV, cable, Internet, or cell service, you're probably having some type of noise blaring in your ears and guiding you down the wrong path.

With so much noise telling you how to live, who you should be, how you should act, and what you should buy, you can easily get derailed in your goal to live an authentic life. This goes back to Technology Reboot and Protecting Your Perimeter. In the process of learning how to use technology to suit your life, you also need to learn to drown out the noise attempting to penetrate your perimeter.

Remember that all websites, news shows, TV shows, and Internet shows all rely on one thing: ratings! They care about you as long as you're contributing to their media outlet. The best way to get ratings is to be controversial. If you can understand their motivation, then you can understand how confusing their messages can be.

Even while you're attempting to control the messages in your own life, there's simply too much noise when you leave the confines of your own perimeters. These messages are shot at you like flaming arrows toward your heart. Learn to drown out the noise you see and hear, and don't let it ever distract you from living a better life. In knowing who you are, you no longer have to live in survival mode believing what others expect of you.

Relying on Authenticity

Once you find a place of authenticity, then you need to live authentically in every aspect of your life. In living a Thrival Life, you're going to be exposed to inauthenticity whenever it rears its ugly head—whether in media, social media, or even among your friends. You'll begin to see how they're living with survival syndrome instead of a thriving life.

Never let anyone or anything drag you back down into an inauthentic life. Some will try, mainly out of jealousy, because they want what you have discovered, but are unwilling to work for it or don't know where to begin. They might think it's some magical concoction, but it's not. You have simply taken the time and put in the effort to get to a place of authenticity. Give others grace in their confusion, but never let them bring you back down.

Stop living an unnatural life and return to the authentic life we were created to live. The more authentic you are, the more you will create authentic content. Authenticity is not some goal you attempt to obtain; rather, it comes from being an authentic person. The peace found in living from your own space is inexplicable. Never miss an opportunity to embrace true authenticity.

22

FANNING THE FLAMES

Creating Space for Greater Impact

"From a little spark may burst a flame."
~ Dante Alighieri

There is something magical about a campfire. When the flames dance upon the crackling wood against a quiet backdrop of a dark night, there is little to do except talk and make S'mores. I think many issues and problems could be solved and relationships strengthened if we spent more time around campfires. All major negotiations and difficult conversations should happen around a campfire. The end result would probably be more beneficial to both sides.

The challenge with campfires is they always need to be stoked. You can't simply build the fire and then walk away. The longer you are away from the campfire, the less light and heat it will produce until it eventually burns out. But if you stay by the fire, fan the flames, and add wood, you can create a captivating fire with enough light and heat for numerous people to enjoy throughout the night.

Fan the Flames

Living a Thrival Life will always produce a few road bumps along the way. You will get distracted, get tired, ask "What's the point," or get discouraged. It's important for you build a solid process to keep fanning the flames.

Hopefully, what has been made clear in this book is the fact there are numerous forces at work against you. They're not all intentional, but they will extinguish your flame and derail you from your Thrival Adventure if you let them. Coming in the form of distractions, negativity, overwhelmed schedules, or self-doubt.

In order to combat this issue, you need to be aware of what's happening around you. You need to be proactive in creating space for you to pursue your Thrival Adventure. If you're not intentional about creating this space, then your flame will eventually be extinguished. Your flame has to be stoked and fanned consistently to keep its intensity.

I like to steal away to quiet places in the midst of major creative projects. In the quiet without distractions, I can truly fan the flame for long periods of time. The light and heat it produces allow for longer periods of productivity. When I try the same process at home or in an office, I'm constantly being pulled away by distractions.

Each time I'm pulled away from the flame, the fire slowly begins to burn out. By the time I return to my project, I have to spend more time and energy building the flame back up to where I left it before the interruption—time and energy I could have poured directly into my Thrival Adventure. Cherish your flame and understand its power in your ability to create and complete your goals.

Create Space

In order to live a Thrival Life, you're going to have to learn to create space for your Thrival Adventure. This is a specific set-aside, concentrated time dedicated to working toward your goal. Find the rhythm for your flame to burn bright. This time will not happen on its own, and it's not good to simply take the little time or spaces available. You may need to wake up an hour earlier or stay up an hour later. You might need to steal away to some quiet place over the weekend.

Your "space" will look different than others, depending upon the direction your Thrival Adventure is pointing. The reality is no matter how good your work might be, it will never see the light of day unless you create space for it to be completed.

As I mentioned earlier, I wrote my first book from my recliner. When I started working on this book, I got a desk and some nice monitors to be more "professional" in my writing. As I sat at my desk day after day attempting to push through the manuscript, I realized I simply wrote with more ease in the recliner. This was the place I could more easily fan my own flames.

I don't know why—the recliner is nothing special. But I had better focus and was less distracted when working from the recliner. Your space may be more than time, it could be a place you need to protect or go to in order to create. It could be a shack out back, your favorite coffee shop, or the library. Where it is doesn't matter as much as it is a place where you can fan your flame. The little things are extremely important in the pursuit of your Thrival Adventure, which means you must create the right space for your work to transpire.

Keep Moving

Sometimes you find yourself in a situation where your only option is to keep stepping forward. You don't know what the next step will look like, or where it'll even take you, but you need to keep moving forward.

When met with challenges in our pursuits, we tend to focus on what cannot be accomplished. During these times, you simply need to take a single step. Then another one. Move forward no matter what, so you don't remain stagnant.

If you're in the midst of or about to start a new journey, here are some ways to keep moving forward and put one foot in front of the other.

Take a Step

Take a step forward—the movement forward is absolutely important. If you ever stop, even for a brief moment, you'll be tempted to quit. The momentum you gain by moving forward can keep you rolling even during times you may not know the next step. As entrepreneur Victor Kiam once stated, "Even if you fall on your face you're still moving forward." This progression is the most important point in getting you closer to your goal of a Thrival Life.

Do Not Be Afraid to Backtrack

You may move forward and realize you're not quite in the place you want to be. Don't be afraid to backtrack;

it's all part of the process. The time was never wasted and there was always a nugget of information to learn, especially if you want to repeat this process in the future. You learned something not to do next time. Or you learned how to repeat a task more efficiently in the future.

When you do have to backtrack, make sure you're taking the time to reflect on the experience. Write it down and incorporate it into your notes in order to use the experience wisely.

You Are Going to Fall Down

When you're walking through a place you've never been before, it's inevitable that you're going to fall down, or that you're going to fail … but this is not destructive. How you fall matters less than your ability to get back up and continue with your journey. Again, you need to always have your Thrival Adventure in front of you to achieve your dream. But some days, you may only need to concentrate on the next step.

The only failure is one you do not get up from. If you fall down and don't get up, then you have given up on your dream. There will be tough times and distractions. Before you start, get it in your head that the journey will be challenging. Remember how much you don't want to live in survival mode, and then commit to always getting up no matter what you encounter. You always want to be in a place to take another step.

Enjoy the Experience

If you go through this process head down, you're going to miss many of the wonderful opportunities happening along the way. You can't enjoy the scenery along a beautiful hike if you're only staring at your feet. Your journey will be tough, but it can also be extremely enjoyable. You need to have your head held up in order not to miss these experiences.

If this is a new area for you, then you'll be encountering a series of firsts. Don't forget to enjoy the experience. Celebrate the milestones of the project or process, especially with others. Whatever your goal, don't miss the opportunity to celebrate the small victories. You'll never have these "firsts" again and they are worth celebrating. These milestones are also encouragement to take the next step.

Don't Forget to Look Back

When you take your steps forward, you also need to remember to look back. Have you ever been on one of those pretty grueling hikes, where your endurance was almost stretched to the limit? But then when you looked back down the trail, you realized you have covered an incredible distance.

The same is true with what you create. Although the process might be taxing, when you take the time to review the ground you have covered, it can be pretty amazing to see how far you have come.

When you feel stuck or feel like you can't go on, then take a little time to reflect on the ground you have covered. If you're already pretty far up the mountain, you don't want to turn around before reaching the top. Take the time to see how far you have come and use the motivation to take the next step.

Never discount your dreams, but also, never think they're just going to be laid in your lap. You're going to have to work hard and put in the effort, but the journey itself is well worth the work. Find your dream, create a plan, dig deep, and then start taking the steps. Fan your flames to ensure your light never gets extinguished so you can travel the greatest journey you can imagine.

CONCLUSION

BECOMING A THRIVALIST

"My mission in life is not merely to survive, but to thrive; and to do so with some passion, some compassion, some humor, and some style."
~ Maya Angelou

Stop looking at life as something to *survive*. There is so much more to life, but it's going to be up to you take the first step toward change.

After writing *The Raging Sloth*, I began engaging in many conversations with individuals who were stuck, distracted, and confused. They were not specifically dealing with chronic pain or overbearing limitations; they simply didn't like where they were in life. They wanted success or change, and some even had great plans. But they had no idea how to lighten the load or eliminate the distractions in order to move forward productively. They needed a roadmap.

The Thrival Guide is the answer they had been looking for, and it can help you too. It is a roadmap that leads you out of survival mode. It reminds you there is more to life than simply getting by. It will show you there's a better way—if you're willing to commit to the process.

Your life may be chaotic, your career may be lack-luster, and your relationships shallow. You may have a longing desire to make a greater impact in your life and this world, but you don't know where to begin. Or maybe life is good—you like your job, your family is great, and things are going well—but you feel, deep down in the pit of your soul, there's something more out there. There's someplace where you could make a bigger impact, but you don't have any idea how to take the first step.

The distractions in life are overwhelming and have been hidden so long you never realized their impact on your life.

You're tired of simply surviving the monotony of life. You desire transformation in your own life and deep change in order to make an impact on those around you. This is the Thrival Life!

Your overall goal in life regardless of your Thrival Adventure should be to become a Thrivalist—an individual who goes through life with passion, compassion, humor, and just a little bit of style. Stop living like everyone else in survival mode. Start living a life that is healthy, life-giving, and thriving.

A Thrivalist makes the most out of life because they know they own their own journey. They're in charge of their life and are eliminating any and all distractions which keep them from living a full life.

The world is waiting and desperately needs your Thrival Adventure—the good work only you can bring. Stop surviving life and choose the Thrival Life!

APPENDICES

APPENDICES

DISCUSSION QUESTIONS

Chapter 1: The Evolution of Our Modern Problems

1. Have you ever thought about the amount of information you consume? What comes to mind?
2. What do you do with all the information you consume? Is it truly helpful or distracting?
3. Do you overanalyze purchases, trips, or opportunities? In the end, is the analysis helpful?
4. How has analysis paralysis been a negative factor in your life?
5. How much would you say you worry during any given day? What do you mainly worry about?
6. How often does your worry turn into stress or anxiety over circumstances?

Chapter 2: The Unforeseen Obstacles

1. What External Problems do you think about? How much time do you spend thinking about these problems? How much stress does it add to your life?
2. Have you thought about the stress or anxiety Extension Problems can cause in your life?
3. How do your own expectations cause unneeded stress in your life?
4. Are you good at handling Emergency Problems? Why or why not? What is one thing you could do better in an emergency?
5. How do Everyday Problems affect your life? Do you deal with them well? Are there ways to eliminate them or soften them?

6. If you look at the wheelbarrow you're pushing in life, how full is it getting? Have you ever taken the time to recognize the weight of your burden and the impact on your life?

Chapter 3: Deviating from the Trail

1. How much time do you spend on news and social media sites? Describe your emotions immediately after viewing these sites.
2. What is your relationship with technology? Do you always have to have the latest toy? Why?
3. What confusion does culture cause in your own life? What is one step you can take to better address the issues you face?
4. Have you ever sat down to figure out why you need to do things your way?
5. Do you struggle in asking for help?
6. When you look over your life, how do you think you have veered off the trail and how can you make your way back on the trail?

Chapter 4: Lack of Preparation

1. How well do you think you have been prepared for life?
2. Do you look at adulting as a noun or a verb? Something you do or something you are?
3. What are the lasting effects in your own life and in your family's when you're not properly prepared for life?
4. What are some specific steps you can take in order to begin to properly prepare for life?

5. What are some specific areas of your life that you prepared for with gusto? Areas you invested a lot of time and money?
6. What is stopping you from investing time and money into your life in general?

Chapter 5: Side Effects

1. What are some of the small stresses you deal with?
2. What are some of the major stresses in your life?
3. How does your body react to stress?
4. How have your relationships been affected by stress?
5. How do you deal with your current stressful circumstances?
6. What is one step you could take to deal with your stress more effectively?

Chapter 6: Survival Mode

1. Do you feel you need to numb yourself at the end of the day?
2. What are you numbing yourself from?
3. What avenues are you pursing to numb yourself from the pain?
4. Do you truly believe there's a better way to deal with these pains in life in order to stop surviving?
5. What is the first step you need to take toward a Thrival Life?
6. If you have experienced the suicide of a close friend or family member, what feelings and emotions were stirred up from the event?

Chapter 7: Creating a Better Journey

1. How can you use the Thrival Code as guardrails in your pursuit of a Thrival Life?
2. What is your Thrival Charge?
3. Can you define your Thrival Adventure?
4. What do you need to do to pursue your next Thrival Adventure toward a specific goal?
5. How will you use your Thrival Charge when circumstances do not turn out as planned?
6. What other tools would be useful for you in attempting to pursue a Thrival Life?

Chapter 8: Preparation

1. How is your life not working for you?
2. How are you attempting to live a modern life with outdated ways?
3. Does your M.O. seem outdated? Why?
4. How do you need to change your M.O.?
5. In what area of your life are you just surviving? How can that area be optimized?
6. In what area do you need to take responsibility for your own life?

Chapter 9: Planning Your Route

1. Do you think you can multitask well?
2. What distracts you in the midst of doing work?
3. What is one way you need to be more strategic in your life?
4. How can a schedule be more beneficial in being strategic with your day?

5. What tasks do you need to eliminate from your day or life?
6. What is a habit, addiction, or distraction you can say no to today?

Chapter 10: Impactful Trailblazing

1. What is a bad habit in your life that you would like to change?
2. Do you understand the cue causing your bad habit?
3. What better habit could you substitute in place of the bad one when you have the cue?
4. What discipline will you need to insert in order to create the new habit?
5. How can consistency and focus aid you in creating a new habit?
6. What is your plan to create a new habit?

Chapter 11: Becoming a Trail Guide

1. What do you think about when you hear the term *being boundless*?
2. Do you see the need in serving others around you? What does it offer you?
3. How are you currently serving others?
4. How could you better serve others in your community?
5. Do you feel like you need a mentor or wise sage to speak into your life?
6. What steps can you take to find a trusted guide to help you in your journey?

Chapter 12: Intentional Wandering

1. How have you done intentional wandering in your life?
2. What did you learn from the experience?
3. What is an activity that excites you but which you have not tried before?
4. What is one step you can take today to begin another journey of intentional wandering?
5. How can you hone your skills to make this Thrival Adventure more worthwhile?
6. What can you do to make the most of your time in intentional wandering?

Chapter 13: Staying on the Trail

1. What is the greatest distraction you can identify in your life?
2. Are you being distracted by circumstances, health, or relationships?
3. When you categorize your distractions, where are most of them sitting?
4. What is one distraction you could eliminate today?
5. What is a distraction that's going to take time to eliminate?
6. What distractions are keeping you from your Thrival Adventure?

Chapter 14: Knowing When to Break Camp

1. Where are you complacent in your life, career, or relationships?
2. How can you combat your complacency?

3. What target do you need to set in order to combat your complacency?
4. What fear do you need to control to take the first step?
5. What risks are you going to have to take to move out of complacency?
6. Write down one small win you can achieve to build your confidence.

Chapter 15: Pack Light

1. Do you tend to over pack on trips? Why?
2. Do you completely know and understand your relationship with money?
3. What is your "sucker spot"?
4. What is one item of the "Simplify Life" list you could incorporate today to eliminate some stress?
5. What is one area of your life you could purge? (Hobby, closet, garage, storage facility)
6. During the next Christmas or birthday, what experience could you engage in with others instead of buying stuff?

Chapter 16: Protecting Your Perimeter

1. How is negativity and negative messaging affecting your life?
2. What steps can you take to shut down hate in your life and online?
3. How can you be more positive today? Maybe just put a smile on your face no matter what is happening around you.

4. How is comparison a distraction in your life? What can you do about it?
5. Have you let social expectation dictate how you live life and what you purchase?
6. In what one way can you be flexible in your life and pursuits?

Chapter 17: Navigating the Terrain

1. How would you describe your relationship with technology?
2. List specific ways technology is affecting your life negatively.
3. How is technology affecting your family, work, relationship, or rest?
4. What are some steps you can take today to control technology use in your life?
5. Do you have a technology plan?
6. When are you going to start a Technology Diet?

Chapter 18: Being Resourceful

1. Do you think you're a creative individual?
2. How has creativity served you well in the past?
3. How can you change your environment in order to help hit your target?
4. What is something new you can try that can help you take a risk and grow more confident?
5. What is something you can quit today?
6. How can journaling help you specifically on your journey? By the way, go out and buy a journal right now if you don't have one.

Chapter 19: Enjoy the Journey

1. Have you ever meditated?
2. How do you think meditation could be an asset in your current existence?
3. Do you ever take time to reflect upon your life?
4. How can you do a self-check? What do you need to reflect upon?
5. What did you learn from your successes over the past year?
6. What can you learn from your failures over the past year?

Chapter 20: Setting Your Pace

1. What fears do you face?
2. Do you have FOMO? Why, and in what areas?
3. What areas of your life do you consistently procrastinate?
4. Have you thought about what your rhythm looks like?
5. What do you need to do in each specific area to truly set your own pace?
6. How will responding to each of these areas help you work toward your Thrival Adventure?

Chapter 21: Embracing Your Adventure

1. How do you define authenticity?
2. Can you recognize the inauthenticity in your culture?
3. Define some inauthentic traits you see around you. What is your reaction to these traits?
4. What is the noise that blares inauthenticity?
5. How can drowning out the noise help you live a more authentic life?

6. What is the first step you need to take to live a truly authentic life?

Chapter 22: Fanning the Flames

1. How will fanning the flames help your Thrival Adventure?
2. How do you need to create space in your life to deter distractions and concentrate on your Thrival Adventure?
3. Can you think of a time where you paused on a project only to never finish?
4. Do you give yourself enough grace when you fail to get back up?
5. Reflect upon a time where the experience was grueling yet worth the effort. Why did you put yourself through the experience?
6. What can you learn by reflecting upon those successes and failures in your pursuit of your Thrival Adventure?

Conclusion: Becoming a Thrivalist

1. What is keeping you in survival mode?
2. What is stopping you from living a Thrival Life?

ACKNOWLEDGEMENTS

To my wife Erica, thanks for believing in my dreams and pushing me to be more than I could have imagined. This journey has only been brighter with you by my side.

Thanks to my children, Dylan, Jude, and Presley, for the late-night laughs, fun adventures, and long (sometime weird) conversations. You have added to my life in more ways than I could ever have imagined.

To my mom, dad, and sisters Tammy and Tonya for supporting me and encouraging me through difficult times, then pushing me to pursue a life beyond imagination. The foundation I received from my family has truly been a gift.

A wholehearted thanks to Kary Oberbrunner for believing in me. Without Kary's help and support, none of my writing would have seen the light of day. You are truly an inspiration to many by igniting our souls.

Thanks to Precy Larkins for your detailed edits and suggestions. You help shape a good concept into a great book.

Thanks to Nanette O'Neal for your many suggestions and critiques. They were all invaluable in the creative process. You added much needed color to bland places.

As always, thanks to Suzanne Harrold for helping me feel comfortable, and look good enough, to publish. I am always grateful.

ENDNOTES

Introduction

- "Ryan Holiday Quotes," BrainyQuote.com, http://bit. ly/2gto3q0, accessed on September 17, 2017.

Chapter 1: Evolution of Our Modern Problems

- "Stress Quotes," WiseOldSayings.com, http://bit.ly/2x-vm3rZ, accessed on August 21, 2017.

- Shea Bennett, "Social Media Overload – How Much Information Do We Process Each Day," Adweek. com, accessed October 10, 2017.

- Richard Alleyne, "Welcome to the information age – 174 newspapers a day," TheTelegraph.com, http://bit. ly/2xxaM5K, accessed on October 10, 2017.

- "List of breakfast cereals," Wikipedia.com, http://bit. ly/2wMNARc, accessed on October 10, 2017.

Chapter 2: The Unforeseen Obstacles

- Scott Adams, "Problems Quotes," BrainyQuote.com, http://bit.ly/2xxsFkl, accessed September 23, 2017.

- Tanza Loudenback, "The 10 most critical problems in the world, according to millennials," BusinessInsider.com, http://read.bi/2kFf0XB, accessed on October 10, 2017.

- A.J. Feather, "Top 15 Issues That Have Americans Worried," ABCNews.com, http://abcn.ws/2fZ0g0y, accessed on October 10, 2017.

- Raymond F. Hanbury, PhD, ABPP and Eva D. Sivan, PhD, "Managing traumatic stress after the hurricanes," **American Psychological Association**, apa.org, http://bit.ly/2kEI7u8, accessed on October 2, 2017.

- Joseph Goldberg, MD, "Causes of Stress," WebMD.com, http://wb.md/2yexFP4, accessed on October 10, 2017.

Chapter 3: Deviating from the Trail

- "Vivian Greene Quotes," Goodreads.com, http://bit.ly/2wMtmHq, accessed on September 23, 2017.

- Nick Bilton, "The American Diet: 34 Gigabytes a Day," **The New York Times, NYTimes.com,** http://nyti.ms/2xxDao4, accessed on October 10, 2017.

- Edmund DeMarche, "Antifa Leader, teacher Yvonne Felarca arrested at 'empathy tent' Berkley brawl," Fox News, FoxNews.com, http://fxn.ws/2xxxACp, accessed on September 29, 2017.

- Jeremy Fowler, "Steelers, Seahawks, Titans remain in locker room during national anthem," ESPN.com, http://es.pn/2gtqnO, accessed on on October 4, 2017.

- Chris Bergland, "What Inhibits Eye Contact During Emotional Conversations?," Psychology Today, PsychologyToday.com, http://bit.ly/2y8NqHT, accessed on October 10, 2017.

- Vivek Murthy, "Work and The Loneliness Epidemic," Harvard Business Review, hbr.com, http://bit.ly/2yWg4sk, accessed on October 10, 2017.

Chapter 4: Lack of Preparation

- Benjamin Franklin, "Quotes About Preparation," Goodreads.com, http://bit.ly/2wMXCly, accessed on October 10, 2017.

Chapter 5: Side Effects

- Matt Bevin, "Effects Quotes," BrainyQuote.com, http://bit.ly/2gt4m1z, accessed on *September 23, 2017*.

- "Stress Facts," Global Organization for Stress, gostress.com, http://www.gostress.com/stress-facts/, accessed on October 10, 2017.

- Dennis Thompson, "More Americans suffering from stress, anxiety, and depression, study finds," CBS News, http://cbsn.ws/2jWZLtd, accessed on November 24, 2017.

- "Stress In America: The State of our Nation," American Psychological Association," http://bit.ly/2ziGRzH, accessed on November 23, 2014.

- Bob Beaudine, *2 Chairs: The Secret That Changes Everything*, (Franklin, Tennessee: Worthy Publishing, 2016).

- Maura Kelly, "An Anxiety Epidemic is Sweeping The US," BusinessInsider.com, http://read.bi/2ka7K3X, accessed on October 10, 2017.

- "Depression Statistics," HealthLine.com, http://bit.ly/2yeSgT9, accessed on October 10, 2017.

- Laura Newcomer, "Is Stress Hurting Your Relationships, Here's How to Fix It," DailyBurn.com, http://bit.ly/2kEoGSj, accessed on October 10, 2017.

- David S. Krantz, PhD, Beverly Thorn, PhD, and Janice Kiecolt-Glaser, PhD, "How Stress Affects Your Health," American Psychological Association, apa.org, http://bit.ly/2yXtjt8, accessed on October 10, 2017.

- Mayo Clinic Staff, "Stress symptoms: Effects on your body and behavior," MayoClinic.com, http://mayocl.in/2xvEcpF, accessed on October 10, 2017.

- Joseph Goldberg, MD, "The Effects of Stress on Your Body," WebMD.com, http://wb.md/2gahEDe, accessed on October 10, 2017.

Chapter 6: Survival Mode

- Akira Kurosawa, "Survival Sayings and Quotes," WiseOldSayings.com, http://bit.ly/2wLGdtl, accessed on October 10, 2017.

- Camila Domonoske, "Drinking On The Rise In U.S., Especially For Women, Minorities, Older Adults," NPR.com, http://n.pr/2wN1YsU, accessed on October 10, 2017.

- Jessica Firger, "Prescription Drugs On The Rise: Estimates Suggest 60 Percent Of Americans Take At Least One Medication," Newsweek, newsweek.com http://bit.ly/2ybpkd5, accessed on October 10, 2017.

- Alice G. Walton, "People in The U.S. Are Drinking More Alcohol Than Ever: Study," Forbes Magazine, Forbes.com, http://bit.ly/2yeLqNq, accessed on October 10, 2017.

- Bridget F. Grant, PhD; S. Patricia Chou, PhD; Tulshi D. Saha, PhD, "Prevalence of 12-Month Alcohol Use, High-Risk Drinking, and DSM-IV Alcohol Use Disorder in the United States, 2001-2002 to 2012-2013," The

JAMA Network, JAMA Psychiatry, http://bit.ly/2h-Qa7ql, accessed on November 23, 2017.

- Alexandra Sifferlin, "Why Americans – Especially Women – Are Drinking More Alcohol," Time Magazine, Time.com, http://ti.me/2gug6Bg, accessed on October 10, 2017.

- Denis Campbell, "NHS figures show 'shocking' rise in self-harm among young," TheGuardian.com, http://bit.ly/2kEHnVP, accessed on October 10, 2017.

- Lara Korte, "Youth suicide rates are rising. School and the Internet may be to blame," USA Today, USAToday.com, https://usat.ly/2i0zcm1, accessed on October 10, 2017.

- "Suicide attempts among young American adults on the rise, study says," Fox News, FoxNews.com, http://fxn.ws/2g0txl9, accessed on October 10, 2017.

- "Chris Cornell," Wikipedia.com, https://en.wikipedia.org/wiki/Chris_Cornell, accessed on October 1, 2017.

- Kory Grow, "Chester Bennington's Last Days: Linkin Park Singer's Mix of Hope, Heaviness," Rolling Stone Magazine, RollingStone.com, http://rol.st/2hADD2U, accessed on October 10, 2017.

Chapter 7: Creating a Better Journey

- Joanna Gaines, "Quotes About Thriving," Goodreads.com, http://bit.ly/2yXIYbB, accessed on October 10, 2017.

- Mark Divine, Unbeatable Mind, (Middletown, Delaware: Mark Divine, 2015), 29.

- Philippians 4:13, NLT

- Andrew Snavely, "Every Man Should Have a Personal Code of Conduct: Here Are 2 Great Examples," Primer.com, http://bit.ly/2y9CCa6, accessed on October 10, 2017.

- Gregg Swanson, "What is Your Personal Code of Honor," WarriorMindCoach.com, http://bit.ly/2wLHu3u, accessed on October 2, 2017.

Chapter 8: Preparation

- Pablo Picasso, "The Purpose of Life," QuoteInvestigator. com, http://bit.ly/2hzdlhq, accessed on October 10, 2017.

- Brett Steenbarger, "Living Life With Renewed Energy: The Purpose of Purpose," Forbes Magazine, Forbes. com, http://bit.ly/2gav4z9, accessed on October 10, 2017.

- Julia Halpert, "Why You Need a Purpose in Life," The Wall Street Journal, wsj.com, http://on.wsj.com/2w-ME0hk, accessed on October 1, 2017.

- "modus operandi," Dictionary.com, http://bit.ly/2k-DxE22, accessed on October 10, 2017.

- Farrah Gray, "Farrah Gray Quotes," Goodreads.com, http://bit.ly/2xxROM7, accessed on October 10, 2017.

Chapter 9: Planning Your Route

- Winston Churchill, "25 Famous Quotation About Strategy," TheMarketingTherapist.com, http://bit. ly/2gt7dl4, accessed on October 10, 2017.

- Therese J. Borchard, "Distraction: A Serious Problem of Modern Life," PsychCentral.com, http://bit.ly/2yei-uFJ, accessed on October 10, 2017.

- Daniel J. Levitin, "Why the modern world is bad for your brain," TheGuardian.com, http://bit.ly/2y7qhW9, accessed on October 10, 2017.

- Matt Richtel, "Growing Up Digital, Wired for Distraction," The New York Times, **NYTimes.com**, http://nyti.ms/2hzZUOt, accessed on October 10, 2017.

Chapter 10: Impactful Trailblazing

- "Aristotle," Wikiquote.com, https://en.wikiquote.org/wiki/Aristotle, accessed on October 10, 2017.

- Mitzi Dulan, "6 Benefits to Being a Morning Exerciser," HuffPost.com, http://bit.ly/2kCvH69, accessed on October 10, 2017.

- Charles Duhigg, The Power of Habit, (New York: Random House Trade Paperbacks, 2014), 36.

- University of Southern California, "Developing good habits is more important than self-control, study finds," MedicalXpress.com, http://bit.ly/2guczma, accessed on October 10, 2017.

Chapter 11: Becoming a Trail Guide

- Mahatma Gandhi, "Mahatma Gandhi Quotes," BrainyQuote.com, http://bit.ly/2xxOzV1, accessed on October 10, 2017.

- Neal Cabage, "Why Helping Others Is Good Business," Inc.com, http://on.inc.com/2i30LuM, accessed on October 10, 2017.

- Jeffery Hayzlett, "How Serving Others Can Help Make You A Great Leader," Entrepreneur.com http://bit.ly/2yXxi8Z, accessed on October 2, 2017.

- Christine L. Carter Ph.D., "What We Get When We Give," Psychology Today, PsychologyToday.com, http://bit.ly/2xxqmOO, accessed on September 25, 2017.

Chapter 12: Intentional Wandering

- Not All Who Wander Are Lost." Wikipedia.com, Wikimedia Foundation, 27 Sept. 2017, en.wikipedia.org/wiki/Not_All_Who_Wander_Are_Lost, accessed on October 10, 2017.

- Buford, Bob P. Halftime. Zondervan, 2016.

- Seth Godin, "Can you live in a shepherds hut?," Seth's Blog, sethgodin.com, September 10, 2017, http://bit.ly/2yab7Nn, accessed on October 10, 2017.

Chapter 13: Staying on the Trail

- John Maxwell, "Michael Hyatt Posts", MichaelHyatt.com, http://bit.ly/2ygNSUd, accessed on October 11, 2017.

- Vince Lombardi, "19 Wallpapers," QuoteFancy.com, http://bit.ly/2ybZqlQ, accessed on October 11, 2017.

Chapter 14: Knowing When to Break Camp

- Mark Twain, "Mark Twain Quotes," Values.com, http://bit.ly/2gcWTHi, accessed on October 11, 2017.

- Marcus, Bonnie. "5 Danger Signs That Complacency Will Derail Your Career." Forbes.com, Forbes Magazine, 12 Apr. 2013, www.forbes.com/sites/bonniemarcus/2013/04/12/5-danger-signs-that-complacency-will-derail-your-career/, accessed on October 11, 2017.

- Zack Arenson, "Why Being Complacent Will Ruin Your Life," Elite Daily, Elitedaily.com, http://elitedai. ly/2ziEZaK, accessed on October 11, 2017.

Chapter 15: Pack Light

- Thomas a Kempis, "Thomas a Kempis Quotes," goodreads.com, http://bit.ly/2wOv0Zb, accessed on October 11, 2017.

- Caroline Picard, "There Are More Self-Storage Units Than McDonald's in the U.S.," Good Housekeeping, good-housekeeping.com, http://bit.ly/2i6oVot, accessed on October 11, 2017.

- Winnie Hsue, "Recent WSJ Article Examines the Reason Self Storage Companies Are Booming," SpaceWise. com, http://bit.ly/2kFjZrk, accessed on October 11, 2017.

- Jen Smith, "Simplifying Your Life Brings Benefits," Stress Management for Women, http://bit.ly/2i5lWwo, accessed on October 11, 2017.

- Mick Ukleja, "6 Life-Changing Benefits From Simplifying," Leadershiptraq.com, http://bit.ly/2ziGPbE, accessed on October 11, 2017.

- For more information about the New Hope Orphanage in Areiquipa, Peru please visit http://www.peruhope.org.

- R.J. Brown, "P.T. Barnum Never Did Say 'There's A Sucker Born Every Minute," HistoryReference.org, http://bit. ly/2i5baGt, accessed on October 11, 2017.

- Martin Merzer, "Survey, 3 in 4 Americans make impulse purchases," Creditcards.com, http://bit.ly/2yhTr4r, accessed on October 11, 2017.

- Julius Caesar, "Julius Caesar Quotes," BrainyQuote.com, http://bit.ly/2gcLTcT, accessed on October 11, 2017.

- Ilya Pozin, "The Secret to Happiness? Spend Money on Experiences, Not Things," Forbes Magazine, Forbes.com, http://bit.ly/2kGDgbQ, accessed on October 11, 2017.

- Jay Cassano, "The Science of Why You Should Spend Your Money on Experiences, Not Things," Fast Company, FastCompany.com, http://bit.ly/2ydpRvf, accessed on October 11, 2017.

Chapter 16: Protecting Your Perimeter

- H. Jackson Brown, Jr., "H. Jackson Brown, Jr. Quotes," BrainyQuotes.com, http://bit.ly/2yhQsc2, accessed on October 11, 2017.

- Proverbs 4:23, paraphrased.

- Lisa Firestone, Ph.D., "How Negative Thoughts Are Ruining Your Life," Psychology Today, PsychologyToday.com, http://bit.ly/2i5DnwX, accessed on October 11, 2017.

- Adam Hoffman, "Can Negative Thinking Make You Sick?," Health.com, http://bit.ly/2g3gYfv, accessed on October 11, 2017.

- "Nonviolent Resistance," KingEncyclopedia.com, http://stanford.io/2gduuR8, accessed on October 11, 2017.

Chapter 17: Navigating the Terrain

- Albert Einstein, "Albert Einstein Quotes," BrainyQuotes.com, http://bit.ly/2yFy8ez, accessed on October 11, 2017.

- Matt Richtel, "Are Teenagers Replacing Drugs with Smartphones?," The New York Times, **NYTimes.com**, http://nyti.ms/2gyGee9, accessed on October 11, 2017.

- Mia De Graff, "Losing your phone or missing the train 'is as stressful as a terrorist attack'," dailyMail.com.uk, http://dailym.ai/2yanxr1, accessed on October 11, 2017.

- Gavin Fernando, "Four Main Reasons for Gen Y's Unhappiness," news.com.au, http://bit.ly/2kHhK76, accessed on October 11, 2017.

- Eddie Wren, "Can't tear yourself away from the computer? Too much time online can lead to stress, sleeping disorders, and depression," dailyMail.com.uk, http://dailym.ai/2hC2pQh, accessed on October 11, 2017.

- Therese Borchard, "Distraction: A Serious Problem in Modern Life," World of Psychology, PsychCentral.com, http://bit.ly/2yeiuFJ, accessed on October 11, 2017.

- Daniel J. Levitin, "Why the modern world is bad for your brain," The Observer, TheGuardian.com, http://bit.ly/2y7qhW9, accessed on October 11, 2017.

- Amelia Hill, "Boredom is good for you, study claims," TheGuardian.com, http://bit.ly/2ydwQUM, accessed on October 11, 2017.

Chapter 18: Being Resourceful

- Brene Brown, "Brene Brown Quotes," Goodreads.com, http://bit.ly/2ycd9yY, accessed on October 11, 2017.

- "Importance of Creativity," Crayola.com, http://bit.ly/2i5pFKo, accessed on October 11, 2017.

- Matt Batey, Ph.D., "Is Creativity the Number 1 Skill for the 21st Century?," Psychology Today, PsychologyToday.com, http://bit.ly/2i7mlsD, accessed on September 22, 2017.

- Eric Wahl, "The Importance of Creativity in the Workplace," AllBusiness.com, http://bit.ly/2z14hJh, accessed on August, 18, 2017.

- Bob Goff author of Love Does. Bob Goff spoke at a StoryBrand conference in Chicago in November 2015 where he discussed quitting something every Thursday.

- For more information about Sketchnotes visit http://rohdesign.com/sketchnotes/.

Chapter 19: Enjoy the Journey

- Confucius, "10 Powerful Quotes by Confucius That Can Change Your Life," theunboundedspirit.com, http://bit.ly/2wPNB6W, accessed on September 1, 2017.

- Mayo Clinic Staff, "Meditation: A simple, fast way to reduce stress," MayoClinic.com, http://mayocl.in/2w-PKGeG, accessed on August 31, 2017.

- Kevin Loria, "7 Ways Meditation Changes Your Brain and Body," BusinessInsider.com, http://read.bi/2g2fEJD, accessed on August 31, 2017.

- Alice G. Walton, "7 Ways Meditation Can Actually Change Your Brain," Forbes Magazine, Forbes.com, http://bit.ly/2yhTAoi, accessed on October 11, 2017.

- Amelia Hill, "Boredom is good for you, study claims," TheGuardian.com, http://bit.ly/2ydwQUM, accessed on October 11, 2017.

- John Locke, "John Locke Quotes," BrainyQuote.com, http://bit.ly/2gxaqWW, accessed on September 12, 2017.

Chapter 20: Setting Your Pace

- Wayne Gretzky, "Wayne Gretzky Quotes," BrainyQuotes.com, http://bit.ly/2yaLclb, accessed on October 11, 2017.

- Oxford English Dictionary, 2013.

- Kristi Hedges, "Do You Have FOMO: Fear of Missing Out?," Forbes Magazine, Forbes.com, http://bit.ly/2xzTvZp, accessed on September 15, 2017.

- Sundi Balu, "FOMO is Real: Does Your Business Really Need That Shiny New Tech Solution?," Forbes Magazine, Forbes.com, http://bit.ly/2kHtRRt, accessed on September 12, 2017.

- Melody Wilding, "Career FOMO: How to Stop 'Fear of Missing Out' From Ruining Your Happiness," Forbes Magazine, Forbes.com, http://bit.ly/2yagn6e, accessed on September 12, 2017.

- Justin White, "Research find links between social media and the 'fear of missing out'," The Washington Post, washingtonpost.com, http://wapo.st/2xysASJ, accessed on September 12, 2017.

- Michelle Singletary, "One millennial's advice to peers on saving for retirement: Don't live by FOMO," The Washington Post, washingtonpost.com, http://wapo.st/2kHSqOh, accessed on September 12, 2017.

- Nico Lang, "Forget 'FOMO.' This is why you should actually want to miss out on social media," The Washington Post, washingtonpost.com, http://wapo.st/2yd9BtZ, accessed on September 12, 2017.

- Hara Estroff Marano, "Why We Procrastinate," Psychology Today, PsychologyToday.com, http://bit.ly/2ycYBwD, accessed on September 15, 2017.

- Brian Tracy, "7 Great Habits of The Most Successful People," Entrepreneur.com, http://bit.ly/2yes1uq, accessed on September 15, 2017.

Chapter 21: Embracing Your Adventure

- Carl Jung, "Quotes About Authenticity," Goodreads.com, http://bit.ly/2ge52Ls, accessed on September 30, 2017.

- Pamela Engel, "Bill Cosby's sexual-assault trial starts today – here's the backstory of the allegations against him," BusinessInsider.com, http://read.bi/2i5kqdK, accessed on October 11, 2017.

- Abby Phillip and Sarah Larimer, "Jared Fogle charged with paying for sex with minors, possessing child porn," The Washington Post, washingtonpost.com, http://wapo.st/2i5XsTG, accessed on October 10, 2017.

- Sasha Savitsky, "Harvey Weinstein accused of raping 3 women, sexually harassing Gwyneth Paltrow, Angelina Jolie," Fox News, FoxNews.com, http://fxn.ws/2yb37OO, accessed on October 11, 2017.

Chapter 22: Fanning the Flames

- Dante Alighieri, "Flame Quotes," BrainyQuote.com, http://bit.ly/2i3CW6i, accessed on September 20, 2017.

- Victor Kiam, "Moving Forward Quotes," BrainyQuote.com, http://bit.ly/2gc5tpE, accessed on October 1, 2017.

Conclusion: Becoming a Thrivalist

- Maya Angelou, "Maya Angelou Quotes," Goodreads.com, http://bit.ly/2zgLxqt, accessed on October 1, 2017.

THE THRIVAL GUIDEBOOK

Follow along *The Thrival Guide* with assessments, guides, and plans to help you achieve The Thrival Life!

IF YOU LIKED THE BOOK
YOU WILL LOVE THE EXPERIENCE
Join the Thrival Guide Community

Do you want to work directly with Eric Eaton?
Let Eric guide you through eliminating your distractions to live a better story.

Imagine finding purpose and harmony among the chaos of life.

You can join a coaching group, enlist in one of *The Thrival Guide* courses, or join our online community. Participants can join from anywhere in the world.

Why keep living in survival mode when you can live a Thrival Life?

Find out more at
THETHRIVALGUIDE.COM

SPEAKER | AUTHOR

Eric understands the challenge of finding the right speaker for an event, bringing the correct topic, and the importance of engaging the audience. As a consultant, business leader, and former pastor, Eric knows the success of any event can easily hinge on the quality of the speaker.

Eric is keenly aware of the need to engage with the audience, equip them with practical takeaways, and provide a different perspective on creating a better adventure. He customizes each message and training to achieve and exceed the desired objectives of his clients.

Contact Eric today to begin the conversation
ERICPEATONSPEAKER.COM

**Learn more about
KNIGHTS OF HEROES:**

knightsofheroes.org

ABOUT THE AUTHOR

Eric is the author of *The Raging Sloth* and helps individuals and organizations find harmony among the chaos. His desire is to show people how to create a better *adventure* in their own lives so they can live a thriving life. Through his writing, speaking, and coaching, he helps people realize they're not alone in their struggles. By eliminating those distractions keeping you from a better story, you can truly live a thriving life.

Eric started out early in his career blazing a quick trail of success as a consultant. However, a hip reconstruction surgery sidelined him and left him with chronic pain since the age of 27. Eric has spent the last few years helping people deal with their own obstacles and struggles—while realizing many people are weighed down with their own distractions without a path to move forward.

Eric wants to show those who live with limitations that their lives have meaning and purpose. Through his speaking and writing, he is committed to helping people find their own path to a better adventure. Eric and his wife Erica live in the mountains of Colorado and are blessed with three awesome teenagers.

Connect at: EricPEaton.com

CPSIA information can be obtained
at www.ICGtesting.com
Printed in the USA
LVOW13*0041020518

575654LV00006B/71/P